What is The Bible?

JOHN BARTON

First published 1991
Triangle
SPCK
Holy Trinity Church
Marylebone Road
London NW1 4DU

British Library Cataloguing in Publication Data

Barton, John, *1948–*
    What is the Bible?
    I. Title
    220
        1000085919
    ISBN 0 281 04528 3

Typeset by Inforum Typesetting, Portsmouth
Printed in Great Britain by
Courier International Ltd
East Kilbride

Contents

Foreword

Most of this book was written in Bonn, where I spent a sabbatical term staying in the University guesthouse. Connections with Bonn, originally as the result of the joint seminars between the Oxford Theology Faculty and the Protestant (latterly also the Catholic) Theology Faculty there have become increasingly important to me, and I should like to thank all those who made my stay so enjoyable. Though I am of course responsible for the final text, I was greatly helped by two friends who read my manuscript and offered constructive advice, Elizabeth Aldworth and Nicola Mitra (the latter not for the first time). My wife Mary has been a great support to me over the time the book has taken to complete, and it is dedicated to her with love and much gratitude.

John Barton
Oxford, April 1991

Introduction

Castaways on *Desert Island Discs* have always been asked which book they would like to have with them in their exile 'apart from the Bible and Shakespeare' – which are to be provided as a matter of course. Few have had the impertinence to suggest that one (or both) might be removed, to make room for other choices. Desert islands, like libraries, bookshops, and homes, would not be complete without these two enduring parts of the heritage of all English-speaking people.

Yet to put it that way immediately reminds us of the differences between them. Shakespeare comes in many editions, but the words (give or take details of spelling and a few variations) are the same in them all: the English words Shakespeare himself wrote. The Bible was not originally written in English at all, and there are many different translations of it. New ones are appearing all the time. We may be fairly sure that 'the Bible and Shakespeare' in the original constitution of *Desert Island Discs* referred to the Authorised Version (the King James Version, as it is called in America). For that is what 'the Bible' has meant to most English people since the seventeenth century. But it is not necessarily the Authorised Version that you will get today if you ask simply for 'a Bible, please' in a high-street bookshop. You may be offered instead the New English Bible, the Revised Standard Version (or the New Revised Standard Version), the Good News Bible, the New International Version, the Jerusalem Bible (or the New Jerusalem Bible), or the Revised English Bible. Which is 'the real Bible'? Is there such a thing; and does it matter?

Another difference between the Bible and Shakespeare is probably more immediately obvious. Shakespeare is at the heart of English, even world, literature; but no one, presumably, believes that everything Shakespeare wrote is true, or that everything we do should be directed by what we learn from him. People do think this about the Bible. No doubt they would agree that all *translations* of it are more or less imperfect. But the original Bible (in Hebrew, Aramaic, and Greek) is not imperfect: it is the revealed 'word' of God himself. So Christians believe – or so people think they do. And your attitude towards the Bible's religious claims is likely to affect how you feel about lumping together 'the Bible and Shakespeare' as the two chief literary monuments of our culture.

If you are a dedicated Shakespearian, you may wonder why the Bible should be placed in his company. You may agree that the Authorised Version is great English literature, but you may think that is because it is such a brilliant translation. The quality of what was being translated, you may feel, is a different matter. From this literary point of view, King James's translators were doing a remarkable job with an original that left a lot to be desired – like Bach or Mozart, writing superb oratorios or operas with basically weak libretti. Whereas Shakespeare was writing freely, and composing literature that really is great in its own right.

If, on the other hand, you are a religious believer, you may have the opposite feeling. Shakespeare, you may say, is great literature; but the Bible is the word of God. To say 'the Bible and Shakespeare', as if they were the same sort of thing, is an insult to the Bible. A Bible should look and feel different from any 'literary' work, however great, because it *is* different. It should be valued, not because it reads well, but because it contains the words of life.

Buying a Bible confronts us, whether we like it or not, with a choice between these ways of seeing it. For like any other book the Bible comes in a particular physical format, chosen by the publisher to convey a message about what kind of work it is. If you buy an Authorised Version, it may well be bound in leather (or something designed to look like leather). It will probably be on extremely thin paper, with gold edges. And it will be printed in double columns, with the text divided up into individually numbered verses. In short, it will look like no other book in the shop; and its presentation will invite you to believe that it *is* like no other book in the shop – where, indeed, it may be kept in a special glass-fronted bookcase. If you buy a modern translation, it may well be paperback, possibly with pages laid out like a novel, and with a binding to suggest that it is simply a book like any other. You can carry it home unwrapped without anyone suspecting it is a Bible you are carrying.

On closer inspection matters prove slightly more complicated than this. Some modern translations (notably the New International Version) were produced by people with as high a view of the divine inspiration of the Bible as anyone who worked on the Authorised Version, for all that the result of their work comes in a handy paperback format. And, on the other hand, some people whose regard for the Authorised Version is largely at the 'literary' level still prefer it in the formal leather-bound editions they remember from their childhood. (For that matter, they sometimes prefer Shakespeare in a similar format.) Nevertheless the way we print and bind Bibles does convey signals about how we regard them. And there are still taboos about Bibles in modern western society. Even students of religion, who may become entirely used to writing on and even cutting up Bibles for study purposes, are likely to feel qualms about using odd pages from a Bible to wrap sandwiches in. Presenting the Bible so that it looks like just an ordinary book may not always reflect a 'low' view of its divine authority. It may be a clever ploy to persuade people who don't think of themselves as religious that they can buy and read it without compromising their principles, in the hope that, once they do, they will be hooked. So, in fact, it has often proved.

The reader of this book is not being asked to make a prior commitment to any particular view of the Bible. Curiosity is the only precondition. I have tried to answer – without oversimplification but also without needless difficulty – the sorts of questions I think anyone who buys a Bible and intends to read it is likely to ask. It would be disingenuous to pretend that people are likely to buy Bibles if they have no interest at all in religion, or that one can seriously understand what the Bible is about without entertaining any religious ideas oneself. But my aim is not to convert anyone. If the agnostic finds that sooner or later the Bible's claim to religious truth has to be confronted, the Christian believer may, conversely, find that some of what is said disturbs common religious assumptions about Scripture. My purpose is not to convince anyone that the Bible is 'true', but to show that it is profoundly interesting: and that at least some of the questions people ask about it can be answered.

CHAPTER ONE

The Survival of Scripture

Survivors are people who find themselves alive, against all the odds. So to speak of the 'survival' of Scripture is to register that the Bible lives on in our culture when we might expect it to have died out. Modern western society is thoroughly secularised in many ways, and no holy book occupies the central place in people's consciousness that the Qur'an, for example, holds in Islamic societies. Yet the Bible does 'survive' even in a country as secular as Britain. People are still aware of it to a surprising extent.

This awareness, however, is essentially fragmentary. It is most obvious at a literary level, where biblical quotations and allusions are still taken for granted by many writers. A great many common expressions turn out to be biblical in origin, though of course people often do not realise this: the Bible survives in them in an essentially invisible, unrecognised way. Here is a list of examples that can be found in any 'quality' newspaper from time to time, and in many cases in general conversation:

Am I my brother's keeper? (Genesis 4.9)
Making bricks without straw (Exodus 5.10)
Man does not live by bread alone (Deuteronomy 8.3)
The skin of my teeth (Job 19.20)
The valley of the shadow of death (Psalm 23.4)
Three score years and ten (Psalm 90.10)
They shall beat their swords into ploughshares (Isaiah 2.4)

There is no peace for the wicked (Isaiah 48.22)
Holier than thou (Isaiah 65.5)
Can the leopard change its spots? (Jeremiah 13.23)
Wheels within wheels (Ezekiel 1.16)
The law of the Medes and Persians (Daniel 6.12)
The salt of the earth (Matthew 5.13)
Pearls before swine (Matthew 7.6)
The blind leading the blind (Matthew 15.14)
Love thy neighbour (Matthew 19.19)
No room in the inn (Luke 2.7)
It is more blessed to give than to receive (Acts 20.35)
The wages of sin is death (Romans 6.23)
The powers that be (Romans 13.1)
All things to all men (1 Corinthians 9.22)
Fallen from grace (Galatians 5.4)
A labour of love (1 Thessalonians 1.3)

Book titles still use biblical allusions. Elizabeth Smart's
By Grand Central Station I Sat Down and Wept recalls
Psalm 137, 'By the waters of Babylon we sat down and
wept'; John Steinbeck's *The Grapes of Wrath* is an allu-
sion to Revelation 19.15, 'he will tread the wine press of
the fury of the wrath of God the Almighty', which is in
turn reminiscent of Isaiah 63.1–4, one of the sources of
the passage from Revelation. Care is needed here: P.D.
James's popular recent novel (and television serial) *De-
vices and Desires* refers to the General Confession in the
Book of Common Prayer, not to the Bible; and Ernest
Hemingway's *For Whom the Bell Tolls* alludes to a famous sermon of John Donne ('No Man is an
Island . . .'). The fact that expressions from such works
as these can be used allusively, just as can quotations
from the Bible, reminds us how far the Bible has become part of 'English literature'. People know phrases
from it, but very much as they know phrases from the

Prayer Book and literary 'classics'. The Bible has become a part of the shared intellectual culture of the west, not necessarily part of its religious culture. Still, the frequency with which it is quoted certainly qualifies it as a 'survivor', in an age when much other literature from the past is falling into oblivion.

Journalists also commonly assume (but perhaps mistakenly) that their readers are familiar with biblical stories, and use references to them as a kind of shorthand: David and Goliath, the parable of the Prodigal Son, the widow's mite, the conquest of the Promised Land. Educated readers are expected to pick up such references without difficulty. But no one expects people to know which book of the Bible they occur in, nor even, probably, whether they are in the Old or the New Testament. Nor do the stories form part of a connected whole. When people talk about an unequal conflict in which they hope to see the underdog win as a 'David and Goliath' contest, it would be absurd to imagine that they seriously have in mind the part played by David in the history of ancient Israel, or the importance of the story of Goliath in the literary structure of the books of Samuel. It is simply a self-contained incident which serves as a proverbial example of right triumphing over might through divine providence.

The closest parallel to this way of using the Bible is the other major example of 'survival' in our culture: the classical mythology of ancient Greece and Rome. I would guess that detailed knowledge of classical mythology is far more nearly dead than knowledge of the Bible, but allusions to it still crop up. Many people still refer to a ruse by which someone gains entry to someone else's secrets as a Trojan horse; a short and drastic solution to a problem may be described as cutting the Gordian knot; and stories and themes from the myths are still familiar from opera (Orpheus and Eurydice) and painting (the judgement of Paris). But again there is no sense that these motifs form part of a *system*, a coherent whole. Classical mythology and the Bible survive, not as parts of a consistent worldview, but as bits and pieces, half-remembered tales and phrases that stick in the mind but connect with nothing else, not even with each other.

Now it would be easy to say that this is a new situation, a shortcoming of the modern world. We have become more secular, just as we have also lost touch with traditional classical learning. In the process the Bible has turned from a book which was intimately known and grasped in its wholeness, into a few tattered remnants in the ragbag of our culture. We might then go on to make disapproving noises about the impoverishment of the modern western mind.

There would certainly be some truth in all this. If we go back a century or two, we find that writers could assume a knowledge of the Bible (and, for that matter, of classical mythology) of a quite detailed and accurate kind. In 1681 John Dryden published *Absalom and Achithophel*, in which the relations between Charles II, James, Duke of Monmouth, and the Earl of Shaftesbury (Anthony Ashley Cooper) are described by means of a detailed allegory based on the story of David, Absalom and Ahithophel (the more usual spelling now) in 2 Samuel 15–19. It is inconceivable that a poet could assume the necessary biblical knowledge today. People in past centuries knew, not just isolated stories about the ancient Israelites or particular incidents from the Gospels and Acts, but whole connected streams of narrative. They knew in what order Noah, Abraham, David, Hezekiah, and Ezra came in the Old Testament, and which places St Paul visited on his missionary journeys.

They could distinguish between events in the life of Jesus and events mentioned in his parables – which not everyone can do nowadays. More than this, they had a sense of the Bible as a book people actually *read*, chapter by chapter and book by book, because it was not just a compendium of memorable fragments, but a continuous and coherent work with a unified and intelligible message. This was a message, moreover, on which hope for human salvation crucially depended. Such an idea of the Bible of course survives today, but it is a distinguishing mark of committed Christians; it is not a taken-for-granted part of common culture. Along these lines we could well lament the degeneracy of our times – and I could try to make the reader feel guilty for not already knowing everything this book is designed to convey.

But it seems to me that such a series of complaints would be wide of the mark, for two reasons. First, because it romanticises the extent to which even dedicated Christians in past centuries really knew the Bible. To some people it has always been a familiar friend, and so it still is. But for many Christians throughout what we may think of as 'the Christian centuries', the Bible as a central idea (almost a central icon) of Christian faith, may have been extremely important, but its precise content was not necessarily known at a very profound level. Many people in the church of the first few centuries could have told you some stories about Moses, or Abraham, or Job. But they could not have connected these stories together into an ordered historical sequence, any more than most people today can. They could have quoted sayings of Jesus, aphorisms from the book of Proverbs, and comments made by St Paul. But they might have had just as much difficulty as most people today in telling you which was which. It is very doubtful whether most Christians have ever been any better than people today at remembering which incidents and sayings of Jesus occur in all four Gospels, and which in only one, or two, or three. Nor would most Christians in the past have thought that this mattered greatly. For the Gospels existed, they believed, to convey the words of Jesus, and so long as you knew them and tried to live by them, exact scholarly knowledge of the precise contents of each separate Gospel was not required. None of this is meant to suggest that the Bible was not taken very seriously in the past; nor is it meant to treat lightly the consequences (both religious and cultural) of its widespread neglect today. It is simply to remind ourselves that the people of past ages were not always endowed with vast biblical knowledge.

Secondly, in many important respects a modern person's approach to the Bible is almost bound to be different from that of people who lived before the rise of what we may call the 'modern world'. People before about the late eighteenth century tended to know, and take very seriously, the narrative shape of the biblical record. They knew, for example, that Abraham came before Moses, and Solomon after David. But this was partly because the Bible simply was the main source for the early history of the world. Its stories were not 'once upon a time' tales, belonging in children's storybooks. They were the primary historical record of real ancient times, recounting a history which led smoothly into the history of later periods that could be reconstructed from the records of Greece and Rome and then of chroniclers and historians down to the present.

Now it is possible to believe that this was, in fact, a true perception of the matter. Conservative Christians, especially those whom others call 'fundamentalists', do indeed believe it. But it would be foolish not to admit that such a belief is now problematic. No one can believe *as a matter of course* – as if it were simply obvious – that the Bible contains an accurate history of the world. Such a belief can be defended nowadays only by some very subtle and ingenious argumentation, and has become not a naive, but an extremely sophisticated position. In this respect a modern 'Bible believer' is quite different from an early Christian, for whom there simply were no ancient records but the Bible. It would be surprising if the Bible had retained its centrality after the rise of modern historiography, which has so many sources besides the Bible for studying the early history of the human race.

This is to say nothing of the rise of modern science. But science, too, necessarily changes the way the Bible looks to any impartial observer. Nowadays it is commonly said that nineteenth-century scientific discovery (especially the theory of evolution) 'challenged' the biblical account. Certainly that is how many saw it at the time. But whether or not this is correct, clearly there is all the difference in the world between ourselves, if we continue to find Genesis instructive and inspiring *after* we have read about the theory of evolution, and those who lived *before* Darwin and simply assumed, as a matter of course, that the Bible said all that could be known about the process of creation. Christians may say (and I think they would be right) that scientific discovery leaves the Bible just as significant for religious faith as it ever was. But they can scarcely deny that the context in which we now read the Bible is vastly different from that of pre-modern times.

Perhaps, then, it is a surprise that the Bible has survived even as well as it has. And if it is not read as it once was, it is certainly bought. Publishers would not commission the immensely costly translation and

11

retranslation of the Bible which has been going on almost without a break in the present century if they could not be sure that sales would justify their investment. They need not worry. The *Guinness Book of Records* alleges that between 1815 and 1975 2.5 *billion* Bibles were produced worldwide. Even if that is no more than an informed guess, it is known that the Authorised Version sells about 13 million copies every year; and the Good News Bible, a modern translation, sold 110 million copies between 1976 and 1989.

Within the Christian Churches, a significant new development has been the growth of interest in the Bible in the Roman Catholic Church. The reforms of the Second Vatican Council in the 1960s encouraged a much greater use of biblical material in Catholic liturgy, and positively instructed all Catholics (laypeople as well as clergy) to read and study it. It is no longer true that a profound interest in the Bible is the distinguishing mark of Protestant Christians. Catholic biblical translations have led the way in promoting the use of modern English and attention to the best and most up-to-date scholarship. If the initiative has now once again passed out of Catholic hands with the fully ecumenical Revised English Bible, that is only because this is the product of a complete co-operation deriving from a sense that the time for translations tied to particular denominational allegiances has now passed away. Modern British society is pluralist, and this increased interest in the Bible in circles that are avowedly Christian does certainly march alongside the marginalization of the Bible elsewhere. There are plenty of people in Britain today who have never heard of the Prodigal Son or the Sermon on the Mount at all. But the Bible is proving a tenacious survivor; there are plenty of people who would like to give it a fair hearing, and to take it very seriously.

Taking the Bible Seriously

What might it meant to 'take the Bible seriously'? Until the Protestant Reformation of the sixteenth century, no Christian church had ever really defined exactly *how* the Bible was inspired or possessed authority for Christians. People had always agreed in general terms that it should have a central place in the Church's life, but the detail of this had never been the subject of exact definition. And still today it is difficult to find hard-edged definitions of the authority of Scripture which all Christians will agree on. This has not, however, prevented certain popular assumptions growing up about how Christians are 'supposed' to think of the Bible. These assumptions then condition what people expect to find in Scripture, and in some cases make it difficult for them to see what is actually there.

This produces two completely opposite reactions. One is that of the Christian who becomes an enthusiast for the study of the Bible, because of certain clear expectations about what the Bible is 'bound to' contain. When these expectations are disappointed as the Bible is actually read and studied, this sort of person abandons all Christian belief. Too many eggs were being placed in the basket marked 'authority of Scripture', and when the Bible turns out to have imperfections which the theory did not predict, then the baby (to change the metaphor) is thrown out with the bathwater. The other reaction is that of the agnostic who 'knows' that the Bible is certain to contain all kinds of puerile absurdities, and who therefore never reads it in the first place. The first lays on Scripture a weight of expectation it cannot really bear; the other is unwilling to give the Bible a hearing anyway. The answer to both has to be: please *read the text* before you decide what it is going to say. But in a way neither is much to blame, for prevailing assumptions about the nature of the Bible are so powerful that it takes a supreme effort to block them out for long enough to let the text speak for itself. These assumptions are also, in a sense, part of the 'survival' of Scripture: they are the rags and tatters of once influential and complex theories about the Bible, which are still cluttering up the lumber room of the modern mind.

The commonest assumption about the *status* of the Bible is that Christians are required to believe everything in it. To be a Christian, in other words, is to be wholly committed to the truth of the Bible. Thus it is felt to be scandalous if a Church leader is heard to question the truth of anything in the Bible. This is widely seen as almost a *logical* point: Christianity and belief in the truth of the Bible are so much the same thing, that to claim to be a Christian and at the same time to deny the truth of something in the Bible is a sort of contradiction in terms.

In a traditionally Protestant country like Britain there is another side to this. Protestants have usually said not only that everything in the Bible is to be believed, but also that nothing is to be regarded as of the essence of Christian faith *unless* it is in the Bible. Their motto might be 'the Bible, the whole Bible, and nothing but the Bible'. Catholics, traditionally, have been equally committed to the Bible but have always recognised other sources of authority besides, most characteristically the teaching *magisterium* of the church. In Catholic tradition it is thus not a knockdown objection to some doctrinal statement to say, 'But that isn't in the Bible!' Nevertheless the general cultural assumption in this country is still the Protestant one, that (a) everything in the Bible, but (b) nothing else, is of the essence of the Christian faith.

From this assumption about the Bible's status flow further assumptions about its *content*. If the Bible is a wholly true book, then it must contain the kind of material that is capable of being true, that is to say, factual information, and/or statements of doctrine to which Christians are required to assent. This means, in practice, that Christians who see the Bible primarily as a book of truth tend to highlight two sorts of material within it: historical *narratives*, and religious *teaching*. Thus they emphasise the historical books in the Old Testament, such as Genesis, which apparently provide us with information about world history, and (in the New Testament) the historical accounts in the Gospels and Acts. Then they will turn naturally to the Epistles of St Paul, because there above all can be found connected teaching about what Christians are to believe – for example:

> Now I would remind you, brethren, in what terms I preached to you the gospel, which you received, in which you stand, by which you are saved, if you hold it fast – unless you believed in vain. For I delivered to you as of first importance what I also received, that Christ died for our sins in accordance with the scriptures, that he was buried, that he was raised on the third day . . .

> (1 Corinthians 15.1–4)

This picture of the Bible as made up of factual (especially historical) information and religious doctrine is so current in our culture that it is also taken for granted by most people who are agnostic about the Christian faith or hostile to it. Their characteristic reaction is naturally to say that in both areas the Bible is not a book of truth, but a book of falsehood. Its information about the creation and history of the world is largely worthless – the speculations of a pre-scientific and pre-

15

historical culture. 'Creationist' Christians (they say) may put themselves through mental contortions to try and reconcile Genesis with science, but that is just because they have a prejudice in favour of the truth of Genesis – there is no reason why anyone else should take Genesis seriously anyway. As to the religious teaching, that too belongs to a completely outmoded view of the world, in which people believed in angels and devils, in heaven and hell. It has no more claim to *truth* than Greek mythology, and in a modern context is merely picturesque.

Thus attitudes to the Bible are polarised: either you believe every word in it, or you regard it as pure rubbish. It is easy to see that what is lacking here is any discrimination between different parts of the text. After all, there are few large pieces of literature that we treat in such an all-or-nothing way. No other book is expected to be either completely perfect or totally worthless. It does not take much thought to make one wonder whether both Christians and their opponents have not approached the Bible too much with prior convictions about what they will find there, with too little openness to what the text might turn out to contain.

One way of trying to loosen up attitudes to Scripture is to remind ourselves that very large parts of it resist being read as either factual information *or* doctrinal teaching. For example, how is a psalm to be understood, if these are the only available categories?

Create in me a clean heart, O God,
    and put a new and right spirit within me.
Cast me not away from thy presence,
    and take not thy Holy Spirit from me.
Restore to me the joy of thy salvation,
    and uphold me with a willing spirit.

(Psalm 51.10–12)

There are no 'facts' here; no 'information' is being imparted. Equally, there is no religious teaching: the reader is not being told to believe anything about God. The psalm is not in any case addressed to us by God, but by a human speaker to God. It is far from easy to see how we could say that the psalm was either 'true' or 'false', so long as we use those words to refer to factual or doctrinal truth.

Taking our cue from here, we can begin to see that there is a great deal more in the Bible that cannot be brought under one or other of these headings. The parables of Jesus are particularly hard to handle on a 'true or false?' basis. As readers we get caught up in the story, and emerge having learned something about life. But we learn it rather indirectly, and no two people will hear a parable in exactly the same way. How could one say that the parable of the Good Samaritan (Luke 10.25–37), for example, was simply true or simply false? These are not appropriate terms to use.

The same could be said about many other parts of the Bible. For example, in Proverbs there are sayings and aphorisms which were certainly never meant to be read as divine teaching. They are human comments on the human condition and presented as such:

> The sluggard says, 'There is a lion in the road!
>   There is a lion in the streets!'
> As a door turns on its hinges,
>   so does a sluggard on his bed.
> The sluggard buries his hand in the dish;
>   it wears him out to bring it back to his mouth
> (Proverbs 26.13–15).

The New Testament also contains material very hard to classify either as factual 'information' or as divine teaching. In St Paul's epistles there are rulings on particular problems in the churches Paul had founded which are explicitly said to be his own advice, not a commandment from God:

> Now concerning the unmarried, I have no command of the Lord, but I give my opinion as one who by the Lord's mercy is trustworthy . . . (1 Corinthians 7.25).

There are also what seem to be fragments of early Christian hymns, which reflect the early Christians' response *to* God, rather than direction from him:

> He was manifested in the flesh,
> vindicated in the Spirit,
>   seen by angels,
> preached among the nations,
> believed on in the world,
>   taken up in glory. (1 Timothy 3.16).

For the Christian, seeing things in this way may soften and make more subtle the hard lines of a dogmatic defence of the Bible as a book of 'truth'. But for the non-believer, on the other hand, it may serve as a reminder that the Bible cannot plausibly be seen as a book of pure falsehood. Just as the received wisdom among Christians ascribes to the Bible a degree of perfection which experience of it is almost bound to undermine, so the received wisdom among non-Christians caricatures the amount of incredible nonsense to be found in it. People think it contains vast quantities of unintelligible genealogies ('A begat B, and B begat C, and C begat D . . .'), stories that are all about blood and thunder, minute and absurd regulations about sacrifice, and pedantic disputes about obscure Jewish rituals. Agnostics are right, I believe, to highlight such truth as there is in this picture in order to counter excessive Christian claims. But the sober reality is much less scandalous. These elements amount to only a tiny fragment of the whole.

One of the most exciting developments in the last few years for the student of the Bible has been its rediscovery as great literature, by people with no particular religious axe to grind. The power, beauty, and literary skill of books such as Genesis, Job, the Gospels, and the Book of Revelation are on the agenda for literary studies as they have scarcely ever been before. In such circles the Bible is not so much tenuously surviving, as taking on a new lease of life. And this has become possible largely because highly secularised readers of the Bible have been willing to suspend their disbelief, to ignore both claims and counterclaims about the Bible's religious truth, and to examine the text on its own merits. Along such lines some coming together is possible between believers and non-believers, and holds considerable promise for the probably much larger group of people who are neither believers nor unbelievers, but who would like to think that this greatest surviving monument of western religious culture is at least worth reading.

The Canadian literary critic C. Northrop Frye begins his study of the Bible, *The Great Code*, with these words: 'Why does this huge, sprawling, tactless book sit there inscrutably in the middle of our cultural heritage . . . frustrating all our efforts to walk around it?'[1] Its survival may be a joy to the Christian and an irritation to the atheist; it is certainly an invitation to curiosity and to exploration. As we have already begun to see, much comment on the Bible is based on what it is assumed to contain, rather than on an actual reading of it; the impressive statistics of Bible sales do not, of course, tell us anything about how many people actually open the book they have bought. Those who do may be in for some surprises, whatever the expectations they bring to the text. In the next chapter we shall try to give some idea of what these surprises might be.

CHAPTER TWO

The Book and the Books

A printed English Bible looks and feels like a single, unified book. The different 'books' look like chapters or sections; they are all printed in the same way; and (whether the translation is ancient or modern) there is a single style running throughout. Jesus in the Gospels speaks the same kind of English as Abraham in Genesis; the hymns people sing in Revelation (e.g. Revelation 4.11, 5.9, 11.17–18) sound much the same as those in Exodus (e.g. Exodus 15) or the Psalms. When people set themselves to read right through the Bible they seldom think of this as if it were a matter of reading through a *pile* of books, but more as a single task (usually one that peters out around Leviticus). And some may have a dim memory of being told as children that the Bible covers the whole of human history, beginning in Genesis with the creation of the world, and finishing in Revelation with its end, and with the creation of a 'new heaven and new earth' (Revelation 21.1). Like a good novel, the Bible has a beginning, a middle, and an end.

But it did not always look like this. The word 'bible' itself is a perfect illustration of the fact that our unified Bible has a history, and was not always the monolith it now seems. English (like other languages) has borrowed it, via Latin, from the Greek *biblia*, 'books', the plural of *biblion*. We still speak, of course, of the 'books' of the Bible, but at most we think of them as being like the collected works of a single author, like the *Complete*

Works of Shakespeare, divided into Tragedies, Histories, and Comedies, but with consistent line-numbering and a standard pattern of presentation.

However, even in modern times there are reminders that things are not necessarily quite so simple. It is possible, for example, to buy a book containing only the New Testament (separate Old Testaments are less common), or even the four Gospels, or sometimes the Gospels plus the book of Psalms. Churches sometimes have a special book of the Gospels for solemn reading during worship, which is more finely printed and bound than an ordinary Bible. And Christian groups will sometimes distribute copies of a single Gospel as part of an evangelistic campaign. You can get paperback editions taken from the Good News Bible for this purpose, which say on the cover 'Good News according to Matthew/Mark/Luke'.

In Judaism the sense that Scripture is a collection of books rather than a single book is maintained, again, in the liturgical sphere, where the books of the Pentateuch (the five 'books of Moses': Genesis, Exodus, Leviticus, Numbers, and Deuteronomy) have a place of special honour, similar to that of the Gospels in Christianity, and are written on parchment scrolls kept in the sacred 'ark' which has pride of place in the synagogue. Other books of the Bible are read from an ordinary printed text.

We may tend to think of all these practices as if Christians or Jews had begun with a single, unified 'Bible', and then singled out the most important sections for special treatment. But the reality is the opposite of this. The Gospels, or the books of the Pentateuch, did not begin life as part of a larger work and then get extracted from it. Our single, unified Bible resulted from collecting together such books as Genesis or the Gospel according to St Matthew, which originally had an independent existence. This is obvious once one starts to think about it, but it tends to be obscured by such elementary things as the typography of Bibles – which often barely divides one book from the next – and by the common 'biblical English' into which all the books are rendered indiscriminately. The tendency – for which there are important religious reasons – to think of all the books as in some sense written 'by God' also sharply reduces any sense that each has its separate identity. If even Shakespeare's plays have a certain unity of style and theme, how much more would one expect *The Collected Works of God* to tell a single, consistent story!

As soon as we begin to take seriously the fact that (as it is sometimes put) the Bible is a library of many volumes, rather than a single book, we immediately face the question why it contains precisely the volumes it does. The best starting-point here is to observe that even today not all works entitled 'The Holy Bible' in fact contain the same books, or have them in the same order. In the western world Bibles differ according to whether they are Catholic, Protestant or Jewish.

The Bible in Different Traditions

The obvious difference between all Christian and all Jewish Bibles, of course, is that the latter do not contain the New Testament. The New Testament is a specifically Christian work, and all Christian Churches agree on what it contains: the four Gospels (called, strictly speaking, 'The Gospel *according to*' Matthew, Mark, Luke, and John); the Acts of the Apostles; the Letters of St Paul, first those to churches (one to Rome, two to Corinth, one to Galatia, one to Ephesus, one to Philippi, one to Colossae, two to Thessalonica – arranged more or less in order of length), then those to individuals (two to Timothy, one to Titus, one to Philemon); the letter called 'to the Hebrews', which is anonymous (despite the attribution to Paul in the Authorised Version), then the letters of other Apostles (James, Peter, John, Jude); and finally the Book of Revelation, sometimes also called the Apocalypse. The title 'New Testament' or 'New Covenant' (Greek *kainê diathêkê*) indicates the Christian belief that through Jesus Christ God has begun a new relationship with the human race, making a new 'covenant' with mankind just as he had once made a covenant with Abraham and his descendants (see Genesis 15). Consequently, in about the second or third century AD, Christians came to refer to the Jewish scriptures as 'the books of the old covenant', that is, books belonging to God's previous relationship with his people. In recent times many Jews have begun to take exception to this (as they see it) derogatory way of referring to the older Scriptures. But for convenience the terms 'Old' and 'New Testament' remain current among both Christians and Jews. In modern Judaism there are various names for the Hebrew Scriptures, as we shall see.

The differences between Catholic and Protestant Bibles relate to the Old Testament (as illustrated in Appendix 2 on pp. 163–164). The differences are immediately apparent if you compare, say, the Revised Standard Version or Revised English Bible with the Jerusalem or New Jerusalem Bible. In the JB and NJB, which are Catholic versions, the Old Testament contains a number of books which do not appear in the Old Testament of the Protestant RSV or ecumenical REB, where most of them have been shunted off into what Protestants call the 'Apocrypha'. Normally you can buy a Protestant Bible with or without Apocrypha, as you prefer, whereas Catholic Bibles always contain these additional books as an integral part of the Old Testament, arranged so as to stand next to the Old Testament books which they most resemble in type or theme.

Thus the historical books in Protestant Bibles run: Genesis, Exodus, Leviticus, Numbers, Deuteronomy, Joshua, Judges, Ruth, 1 & 2 Samuel, 1 & 2 Kings, 1 & 2 Chronicles, Ezra, Nehemiah, Esther. But Catholic Bibles then add some more 'histories': Judith, Tobit, 1 & 2 Maccabees. (The Greek Orthodox Bible adds also 3 & 4 Maccabees, but of modern Bibles known to me only the New Revised Standard Version includes translations of these.) This historical section of the Old Testament is followed by a number of books containing a mixture of what we might call poems, hymns, aphorisms, and philosophical reflections: Job, Psalms, Proverbs, Ecclesiastes, and the Song of Songs. Catholic Bibles add the Wisdom of Solomon and a book variously known as Ecclesiasticus, the Wisdom of Jesus son of Sira, or Sirach. The third main section of the Old Testament, the prophetic books, has some insertions in Catholic editions: after Jeremiah and Lamentations come some additional appendices to Jeremiah, called Baruch (after Jeremiah's secretary of that name) and the Letter or Epistle of Jeremiah – which, to compound the confusion, is sometimes simply printed as chapter 6 of Baruch.

Two further peculiarities of the Catholic text are that the books of Esther and Daniel are considerably longer than in the Protestant version. The Catholic Esther contains a number of additional visions, prayers, and speeches; while Daniel includes two prayers uttered by the three young men in the burning fiery furnace (the Prayer of Azariah and the Song of the Three Holy Children), and two tales about Daniel: the Story of Susanna, and Bel and the Dragon. Most of the additional books are just the same in the Protestant Apocrypha as they are in Catholic Bibles – only their location is different. But the additional parts of Esther, being of a fragmentary nature, look very strange when detached from the body of the text, as they have to be in Protestant Bibles. Thus 'The Additions to Esther', as they are called in the Protestant Apocrypha, do not make coherent sense unless one reintegrates them into the main text. The JB helpfully prints these sections of Esther in italics, so that one can easily read either the longer or the shorter text as a whole. Better still, the REB prints two complete versions, the shorter one in the Old Testament, the longer one in the Apocrypha – probably the best solution.

There are further minor discrepancies not worth detailing here. It should be noted, though, that the Bible of the Orthodox Churches, while largely the same as that of Catholicism, has a few more additions (Psalm 151, for example), and one omission: it lacks the book variously called 2 Esdras or 4 Ezra, which is usually printed as an appendix to Catholic Bibles though it is an integral part of the Protestant Apocrypha. Indeed, a whole chapter could be written on the names and numbers of books attributed to Ezra (in Greek, Esdras), which vary in Hebrew, Greek, and Latin Bibles, and in translations of these in many modern languages. Hardly anyone can remember them without using a chart.

I hope enough has now been said to convince the reader that the question, 'which are the books of the Old Testament?' is not easily answered. How did this situation arise? To answer this question we have to go back to the first few centuries of the Christian era; and in the process we shall gain a much clearer picture of why the term 'Bible' was originally a plural. We shall also gain considerable insight into how some of the books in the Bible came to be written, and what they are like.

The Biblical Canon

In the period when the New Testament was being written, there was not yet an 'Old Testament' in quite the sense there is today. It is not only that (obviously) that *name* would have been inappropriate; more important, the contents of what would become the Old Testament (or the 'Hebrew Scriptures') were not yet fixed. There was, however, a large body of texts already acknowledged by all Jews everywhere in the Mediterranean world as ancient and authoritative, and these texts are the core of what we now know as the Old Testament.

Pre-eminent among these texts were the five books of Moses, the Pentateuch, which Jews then as now called the 'Torah'. This is a Hebrew word traditionally translated 'law', but perhaps meaning something more like 'code for living well' or 'divine instruction'. Alongside the Torah, which already at the beginning of our era had the special place in Jewish synagogues that it has today, Jews also recognised a large number of other writings which were either ancient or believed to be ancient, and which they referred to as 'the prophets' or 'the prophets and other writings'. The Prologue to Ecclesiasticus, written in 132 BC, says:

> Many great teachings have been given to us through the law and the prophets and the others that followed them, on account of which we should praise Israel for instruction and wisdom . . . My grandfather Jesus . . . devoted himself especially to the reading of the law and the prophets and the other books of our fathers.

There was general agreement about which books stood

at the heart of 'the prophets': the books Christians now
tend to think of as the 'histories' (but which Jews still
call the 'Former Prophets'). These are Joshua, Judges, 1
& 2 Samuel, and 1 & 2 Kings. Alongside these were the
books we still refer to as 'prophets', such as Isaiah,
Jeremiah, Ezekiel, Amos, or Hosea. The Psalms, Proverbs and Job were also recognised and seem sometimes
to have been called 'prophets' too, sometimes not.

The crucial point is that, though everyone agreed that
these books and a few others were definitely 'in', there
were no official rulings to determine that other books
were 'out'. It was not even in principle possible to produce 'a Bible', containing exactly those books which all
Jews accepted as Scripture. Scripture was like a series of
concentric circles fading off into a blurred penumbra,
not a sharply defined block of material with hard edges.
On the one hand, there were many books that various
Jewish groups then thought of with much the same kind
of reverence as books like Job or Isaiah, but which are
not now seen as Scripture by anyone. On the other
hand, particular Jewish communities in the first century
AD may well not have possessed every one of the books
that were to become what we now call the 'canon' of
Scripture – that is, the official list of books recognised as
'Holy Scripture'. Each book was written on a separate
scroll, and some synagogues may unwittingly have had
gaps in their collection.

Occasionally in the New Testament we find references to books that are not now seen as part of Scripture, but which are cited as if they had the same kind of
authority as any other 'scriptural' work. Thus the Epistle of Jude (14–15) quotes from the book called
1 Enoch, and describes it as a 'prophecy', even though
Jews and Christians now agree in excluding it from the
Old Testament (except in Ethiopia, where it is still

greatly revered). 'Scripture' was thus a rather more open-ended category than it is for us. People tended to revere any religious book that seemed ancient and edifying; and of course they had fewer resources than we have for deciding whether books really were as ancient as they seemed. The book of Daniel was almost certainly compiled in the second century BC, but it purports to come from the time of the Babylonian Exile of the Jews, i.e. from the sixth century BC. Jews and Christians in New Testament times generally took it at face value, and thought of Daniel as a contemporary of Ezekiel, with equal prophetic authority.

Now the reason why this fluidity about the limits of Scripture produced the confusing variations between Catholic and Protestant Bibles today is this. During the last few centuries BC, Greek translations of the Hebrew holy books were increasingly needed for the benefit of Jewish communities outside Palestine which no longer spoke Hebrew but had gone over to Greek – by then the common language of the whole Mediterranean world. The first part of the Old Testament to be translated was almost certainly the Torah (a further testimony to its supreme status in Judaism), but translations of the other books followed. Sometimes the Greek translations greatly expanded the original – hence the longer versions of Esther and Daniel. At other times, the translators either abbreviated or (more likely) were translating from a Hebrew text that was much shorter than the one we now have – this is especially the case with Jeremiah. In addition, books which never had existed in Hebrew but were composed in Greek for Greek-speaking Jewish communities, particularly in Egypt, began to acquire the same aura as many of the Hebrew writings. The book called the Wisdom of Solomon, probably written in Alexandria in the first century BC but attributed to King Solomon (just like Proverbs), was very highly regarded, and St Paul seems to have been strongly influenced by it. It is possible that the Jews of Palestine had a more conservative view of the extent of Scripture, and were sometimes cool towards the larger 'canon' of the Jews of Egypt, but this is far from certain: there are no records of any disputes between the two groups on this subject.

Christian groups, whether in Palestine or elsewhere, simply adopted the Scriptures of the local variety of Judaism as their own; and for a couple of centuries they do not seem to have given much thought to the question of exactly which books these were or ought to be. But because the Church very soon became dominated by Greek speakers (the whole of the New Testament is written in Greek), it was natural for them to follow the lead of Greek-speaking Jews, and to treat as sacred the longer selection of books that the latter used. For the first few centuries, therefore, 'the Bible' (or rather 'the books') for the Christian church meant a collection that included all the well-established Greek translations together with the purely Greek books, such as the Wisdom of Solomon. None of the Greek books that have no Hebrew original ever became as important, for Christians or Jews, as the 'core' books such as Genesis or Isaiah; but equally, no one thought of excluding them from the Scriptures.

Thus the Bible of the early Church was the Greek Bible. When the Christian faith spread to Latin-speaking areas, and when Greek waned as the common language of the West, Latin versions of the Bible were needed; and it was the Greek Bible, not the Hebrew original, that was translated into Latin. Only in the fifth century, when Jerome (331–420) set himself the task of producing a fresh Latin rendering direct from the

Hebrew, did the Church have to confront the fact that some of its books did not exist in Hebrew at all. By now, what is more, Judaism had hardened its own position, and had decided rigorously to exclude from its Scriptures the purely Greek books. So Jerome, consulting Jewish authorities, found himself being advised that the Greek books were 'spurious'. His own considered verdict was, accordingly, that the Church should treat them as 'deuterocanonical', that is, as forming a second-best layer in the canon of Scripture. But he still translated them, and went on quoting them in his writings; and the Church at large was not willing to do anything so radical as positively rejecting books that had long been held in such high esteem.

There the matter rested until the Reformation in the sixteenth century. The Protestant Reformers finally revived Jerome's proposal, and decided that only books of the Hebrew canon were to be seen as inspired by God. The deuterocanonical books were set aside and called 'apocrypha', a term which in the ancient Church had referred to the works of heretics or other books that were definitely not scriptural. There were differences of emphasis among the Reformers. Calvin's heirs have generally rejected the Apocrypha altogether; Luther considered them edifying, and some Lutheran Bibles still print them as an appendix. (For that matter, Luther also removed to an appendix James, Hebrews, Jude, and Revelation, but in modern times this decision has not been followed even in Lutheran churches.) The English Reformation kept the Lutheran compromise, and in the Church of England the apocryphal books have always been read in the liturgy (the Alternative Service Book 1980 is the first English Prayer Book ever to provide canonical alternatives for every reading from the Apocrypha); though Article 5 of the Thirty-Nine

Articles of Religion says that 'the other Books (as *Hierome* saith) the Church doth read for example of life and instruction of manners; but yet doth it not apply them to establish any doctrine.' Readers of George Eliot's *Adam Bede* may remember how Adam read the Bible on Sunday mornings:

> You would have liked to see Adam reading his Bible: he never opened it on a week-day, and so he came to it as a holiday-book, serving him for history, biography, and poetry. He held one hand thrust between his waistcoat buttons, and the other ready to turn the pages; and in the course of the morning you would have seen many changes in his face. Sometimes his lips moved in semi-articulation – it was when he came to a speech that he could fancy himself uttering, such as Samuel's dying speech to the people; then his eyebrows would be raised, and the corners of his mouth would quiver a little with sad sympathy – something, perhaps old Isaac's meeting with his son, touched him closely; at other times, over the New Testament, a very solemn look would come upon his face, and he would every now and then shake his head in serious assent, or just lift up his hand and let it fall again; and on some mornings, when he read in the Apocrypha, of which he was very fond, the son of Sirach's keen-edged words would bring a delighted smile, though he also enjoyed the freedom of occasionally differing from an Apocryphal writer. For Adam knew the Articles quite well, as became a good churchman. (George Eliot, *Adam Bede*, chapter 51)

The Catholic Church, however, continued to defend the traditional longer canon. Though it uses Jerome's term 'deuterocanonical' for the non-Hebrew books, it does not in practice accord them any lower authority than the rest of the Old Testament. And there the question remains. The accepted compromise in ecumenical Bibles is to include all the books of the Catholic canon, but to remove them from their position within the Old Testament and print them, under the heading 'Apocrypha', between the Testaments, or occasionally after the New Testament.

One oddity that results from this is that though the Protestant Old Testament contains exactly the same books as the Jewish Scriptures, they are not in the same order. The order is the order of the Greek Bible, with the purely Greek books simply taken out. And the order of the Greek and Hebrew Bibles has never been quite the same – possibly a further indication that they were formed to some extent independently, even though both were a selection from the same large repository of Jewish sacred books. Generally speaking, the Greek (and hence the Christian) Bible arranges the books thematically. There are three basic divisions: history, poetry, and prophecy. The Christian arrangement ignores the special status of the Pentateuch and simply lets the story run on from Moses to Joshua and then down to the age of Ezra and beyond. In the Jewish arrangement there are also three divisions, but there is less evidence of attention to subject-matter. The books of Moses are treated as one thing – Torah, 'instruction'. The other historical and prophetic books, lumped together, are treated as quite another – 'prophecy', which perhaps means 'revealed comment on the Torah' rather than 'prediction of the future', as modern readers tend to assume. The third division of the Hebrew Bible is called by the bland title 'the Writings' and seems to be a ragbag into which everything not deemed Torah or Prophets can be dumped. The three titles, Law (*torah*), Prophets (*nebî'îm*) and Writings (*ketûbîm*) produce the convenient acronym *Tanak* which Jews now sometimes use as shorthand way of referring to their Scriptures; but even this, with its built-in reference to the threefold division, is a reminder that Scripture has remained 'the books' (plural) for Jews in a way that it has not for Christians.

Two things stand out from this brief history of the formation of the Bible. First, Christians have not always had exactly the same books as their Scriptures. The Old Testament has existed in various versions, some considerably longer than others, though with a common core. The New Testament is now agreed by all, but it too has at times been fuzzy at the edges. In the Orthodox Churches of the East, people were sometimes doubtful whether Revelation should really be included, and in the Latin West, whether Hebrews should be. These uncertainties persisted as late as the fourth or fifth century AD. Above all, however, these were uncertainties about a *collection* of books, not all of which every local community might possess anyway (private individuals, unless rich, would be unlikely to possess any of them). They were not questions about the contents of a single, unified Bible. Some scriptural books might have been rated more highly than others – people did not see Scripture as all on one level, as modern Christians tend to do.

The formation of Scripture was by and large not a highly controversial process. There are very few (if any) books now in the Bible that are there because someone decided, against fierce opposition, that they should be included. Even in the few cases where there were disputes, these arose because the books in question were already very highly regarded by many people. If we wished to give a religious interpretation to all this, we might say that the core of the Bible was felt to be somehow self-authenticating. More neutrally, we might say that conservatism was always the most powerful force in the formation of the biblical canon. Certain books had been respected for as long as anyone could remember, and people in the ancient world did not take it on themselves to contradict their forebears. As the second-century Christian writer Origen put it, quoting Proverbs 22.28: 'Remove not the ancient landmark which your fathers have set.'

Who Wrote The Books?

None of this answers the question how the biblical books came to be written in the first place. This is a question which needs to be answered for each biblical book separately, but some broad general principles can be stated. We have no record of the composition of any of the books of the Bible. Early Church Fathers occasionally describe how the Gospels were written, but their suggestions usually reflect legendary tradition, or apparently logical deduction from the texts themselves, rather than real historical information. For example, in the Gospel according to St John, after Jesus has spoken about the destiny of the 'beloved disciple', the text continues, 'This is the disciple who is bearing witness to these things, and who has written these things; and we know that his testimony is true' (John 21.24). So it was assumed that the Gospel must have been written by that disciple – though *these* words, as one can see if one reads them carefully, must logically be by someone else! Logical deduction also produced the conclusion that the 'beloved disciple' was John son of Zebedee, one of Jesus' 'inner cabinet' of Peter, James and John. Thus the stage was set for detailed accounts of how John came to write the Gospel, and explanations of why his Gospel was so different from that of Matthew, Mark and Luke. But while no one can conclusively disprove the theory that this Gospel was written by that particular John, there are many reasons why most modern scholars think it improbable. Even if it is true that traditions in the Gospel go back to the 'beloved disciple', and even if he was indeed John the brother of James, the work shows signs of having been extensively reworked, edited, and adapted to new needs.

This is, in fact, the principal problem in talking about the 'authorship' of almost all biblical books. In the modern world a book is normally by a named individual and published at a particular moment. Borrowing ideas – still more already existing paragraphs or chapters – from other writers, is frowned on as 'plagiarism'; and compositors are expected to copy the author's words exactly, not to adapt them to their own taste. None of these things was true in the ancient world, where books – and especially religious books – 'grew' rather than being written by an individual author. Most of the books in the Bible are the traditional, time-honoured texts of a religious culture which lived by handing on tradition from generation to generation. Only, perhaps, in the case of St Paul are we dealing with a named individual whose authentic letters were transmitted in exactly the form he had sent them to the churches he corresponded with. And even here, some of the allegedly Pauline letters may turn out not to be by the apostle at all, but imitations of his style (Ephesians possibly, the letters to Timothy and Titus probably), while others may be cobbled together from bits and pieces of several different letters (possibly 2 Corinthians, according to some scholars). With the Old Testament prophets we have in each case a core of sayings that go back to the prophet whose name the book bears. But in most of them there are almost certainly swathes of material

added by editors and scribes over the long period between the time of the prophet and the moment when
the book became so venerable that further additions
were regarded as illicit. In the case of the book of Isaiah,
this may be a period of several centuries; for Isaiah lived
in the eighth century BC, but his book was probably not
in its present form before about the fourth.

Apart from the books of the prophets, almost all the
other books of the Old Testament are anonymous anyway. Tradition speaks of the 'five books of Moses', the
'Proverbs of Solomon', and the 'Psalms of David', but
the Bible itself nowhere says that these books were actually composed by the people named. It is more a question of associating certain kinds of people with certain
types of writing. David, according to stories in 1 Samuel, was a talented musician: 'Whenever the evil spirit
from God was upon Saul, David took the lyre and
played it with his hand; so Saul was refreshed, and was
well, and the evil spirit departed from him' (1 Samuel
16.23). This early music therapist accordingly became
the patron of music and hence of psalm-writers, and
many of the psalms bear the heading 'of David'. Solomon wrote and collected proverbs or 'wise sayings'.
(which in the ancient world were normally ascribed to
kings or royal officials): 'Solomon's wisdom surpassed
the wisdom of all the people of the east, and all the
wisdom of Egypt. . . . He also uttered three thousand
proverbs; and his songs were a thousand and five' (1
Kings 4.30–2). So all 'wisdom' (what we might think of
as elementary philosophy) was attributed to him: Proverbs, Ecclesiastes, the Song of Songs, the Wisdom of
Solomon. Moses was seen as the source of all 'torah'
because it was he who received the basic core of Israel's
law – the Ten Commandments – on Mount Sinai. Once
Jews came to think of all the five books of the

Pentateuch as 'law', they attributed them all (not just the legal sections in them) to Moses, and in much later times rabbis would describe any authoritative ruling on a disputed issue as a commandment of Moses from Sinai. This should not be thought of in modern terms, as if the books were, or were seen as, a kind of forgery. It has to be understood in the context of literary conventions different from our own. And in one sense the modern Bible reader can take comfort from it: if we do not know when, where, or how most of the Bible got written, neither did the first generations of Christians. It was simply the traditional religious literature that had come down to them, 'the books', in which the wisdom of the ages was to be found.

CHAPTER THREE

Unity and Diversity

Much Christian thinking about the Bible typically proceeds by trying to make basic assumptions about what the Bible 'must' be like. We imagine what kind of book we would give to the human race if we were God, and wanted to communicate the truth about ourselves. It is quite easy to construct a plausible chain of reasoning which runs as follows: God is perfect and cannot wish to mislead us; the Bible is his self-revelation; therefore the Bible too is perfect and cannot mislead us; therefore everything in the Bible is true, and it is a perfect vehicle for God's communication with us. From this watertight position one can then go on to develop methods for extracting pure truth from the biblical texts.

It will be obvious by now that this is not the point of view from which the reader of this book is being encouraged to approach the Bible. It is no part of my purpose to try and convince the reader that the Bible is deeply *im*perfect, or to treat it with scorn. But I believe one should begin, not from hypothetical ideas about what kind of book God can be supposed to want us to have, but from the observable character of the Bible we have actually got. If it is indeed a divine intention that gave us this book, then that intention must have operated along more winding paths than those implied in the previous paragraph; and God must have wished us to have, not a neat set of definitions, but a large and varied range of books, written at many different times and forming a unified corpus only as the end product of a lengthy process of selection and reception. The religious believer, I would suggest, might get further by asking what kind of God would have wanted us to have the Bible as it now is, than by first assuming that God's character, and therefore his probable intentions, are known already, and then going on to force the Bible into the required mould. In any case this book is not only for religious believers: it is for anyone curious about the Bible. So it is surely more sensible to begin by getting sharply into focus what the Bible is actually like.

In the last chapter we saw that even the exact contents of the Bible are subject to some vagueness of definition. Today the various religious communities that use the Bible still do not wholly agree about what should be in it, and this, it seems, has always been the case. All the different canons of Scripture known to us thus have a certain miscellaneous character. This becomes even more apparent when we start to investigate the nature of the various books that make up the miscellany. It is surely inconceivable that anyone would have deliberately planned *any* of the selections of books that Jews or Christians have called 'the Bible'. They are, as I put it at the end of the last chapter, received texts which have gradually settled into place; they were not compiled by someone operating according to a set of exact principles. However, this should not be taken to imply that the texts are miscellaneous in the sense of sharing no common family likeness. In many ways the very opposite is the case. One of the arguments for certain books being accepted definitively as 'Scripture' was precisely that they so strongly resembled books that were already 'official'. And when biblical translations use a uniform 'biblical English', they do in some ways mislead us by smoothing over marked differences beween various parts of the Bible; but they are not completely off the mark for all that. Biblical books do all have a certain common flavour.

The Bible is Religious Literature

One way of putting this is to note that the books of the Bible all occupy a rather small area within the range of conceivable types of writing: they are all *religious* literature. In a way this is obvious, but it is also important. Ancient Israel must have produced writings that were not religious, and indeed the Old Testament at times refers to such writings: the annals of kings (see 1 Kings 11.41, 14.29), collections of poems (see 2 Samuel 1.18), letters (see 1 Kings 21.8), commercial and legal documents (see Jeremiah 32.9–12). Some fragments of such documents are certainly contained within the books of the present Old Testament. Thus 2 Kings 18.13–16 is probably from an official record; it provides a bare factual statement of what happened when the Assyrians invaded Judah in the time of Isaiah, and it is noticeable that what follows gives a much fuller and more circumstantial account of the same events (2 Kings 18.17–19.37). Numbers 21.14–15 records a poem from the 'Book of the Wars of the LORD', presumably an ancient collection; Jeremiah 29 includes what purports to be an actual letter sent from Jeremiah to his fellow-countrymen in exile in Babylon. But none of the Old Testament books, taken as a whole, *is* a secular document. The only possible exception is the Song of Songs, which is most naturally read as an erotic poem or drama, and which does not appear to say anything at all of an overtly 'religious' kind. It is probable that it came to be regarded as 'Scripture' largely through its association with Solomon – whose writings were, for later generations, automatically sacred – and then interpreted in ways that would generate a religious content. Thus in both Jewish and Christian tradition its erotic imagery has been interpreted allegorically as referring to the relationship between God and Israel, or God and the Church (or, in medieval times, God and the individual soul).

The New Testament is perhaps even more obviously religious literature. Every one of its books exists to convey some teaching about the central religious beliefs of the first Christians: not one is a record of their secular affairs. There is, indeed, an important sociological difference between the literature of the Old Testament and that of the New. Old Testament books are, for the most part, the product of writers living in a nation-state, even though it was a state that at times came much closer to being a 'theocracy' (a nation ruled in theory by God) than most of its neighbours. But the early church was not a state at all, but a specifically religious sect existing within a secular institution, the Roman Empire. Of the two testaments, it is thus perhaps more surprising that the Old Testament should contain no secular literature. But be that as it may, both Testaments are almost entirely concerned with religious topics, and there is little evidence that most of the books in them ever had any other *raison d'être*.

A Single Religious Tradition

Biblical literature all comes from within what is recognisably a *single* religious tradition – or rather a single tradition which then divides into two different but closely related traditions, Judaism and Christianity. The Old Testament, it is true, contains plenty of indications that the people of Israel were not always monotheists who worshipped the God revealed through Moses and the prophets. Within some Old Testament books there may be texts that were originally composed by people who adhered to 'pagan' religions. For example, some of the psalms (e.g. Psalm 29) may go back to prototypes written by the Canaanites, whom the incoming Israelites displaced from Palestine while taking over much of their culture. Some of the sayings and collections of sayings in Proverbs almost certainly originated in Egypt and are translations made by learned scribes in Israel. One lengthy section of Proverbs, 22.17–24.22, is so close to *The Teaching of Amenemopet*, an Egyptian book from (perhaps) the ninth century BC, that the best explanation is that it was translated and adapted from the Egyptian. Many Old Testament laws are part of the common stock of legal material found in most ancient near eastern cultures. The famous *Code of Hammurabi*, from early second millennium Babylon, has many parallels in the Israelite legal code usually known as the 'Book of the Covenant' (Exodus 21–3).

Yet in their present form all the books in which these fragments occur have been thoroughly edited to conform to the mainstream religion of ancient Israel, the precursor of what we now call Judaism. This religious tradition developed and changed very considerably down the centuries, and the religious tone, of, for example, the second-century BC book of Daniel is characteristically very different from that of the (perhaps) ninth-century 2 Samuel. Nevertheless we are still in recognisably the same world, as we would not be if, to take an extreme case, the Old Testament also contained the *Analects of Confucius* or extracts from the *Bhagavad Gita*.

It is important to see that the same is true when we turn to the New Testament. All the New Testament writers are convinced that the God of Israel has done a new thing through the life, death, and resurrection of

Jesus, and that much that was taken for granted in the religious traditions of Judaism must now be modified or abandoned. But it is still the God *of Israel* who has done this new thing – that is, the God to whom the Old Testament Scriptures bear effective witness. Early Christianity was quite plainly a Jewish sect, and one which set great store by possessing the same sacred Scriptures as all other Jews. Of course Christians claimed that they alone possessed the true key to those Scriptures: a claim vigorously denied by other Jews, who came in time to regard them as apostates from true Judaism. But whatever the rights and wrongs of the dispute, the historian is bound to see Judaism and Christianity as branches of a single tree. How widely separated they are or need to be may be discussed; but it has never been plausible to see them simply as two different religions, in the sense that, say, Islam and Hinduism are separate, unrelated religions.

Status of the Biblical Books

The books of the Bible are also all *semi-official* documents of this basically unified religious tradition. Again, we should distinguish the original intention of the biblical books from the status they had come to have by the time they were being regarded as 'the books' recognised by Jews, or Jews and Christians. Much in the Old Testament was presumably composed by private individuals, who did not originally think of themselves as writing 'Scripture'. Similarly, those who first collected and compiled accounts of the life of Jesus – the forerunners of the evangelists, the people on whose work our present Gospels rest – may not have been thinking beyond the next occasion when they would have to tell the story of Jesus to a particular local congregation. (Modern study of the Gospels suggests that it was as material for 'sermons' or instruction that many of the narratives were first fixed.) But long before anyone thought of all the various books in the two Testaments as forming a 'Bible', they must already in practice have acquired a high, more or less official, status. For, as we saw in the last chapter, canonisation was not the decision of Jewish or Christian authorities to adopt books that had previously been of little importance. It was the general, usually tacit, acceptance of what had come down to the religious community from the past.

There are, as a matter of fact, some very diverse voices to be heard within the Bible. In the New Testament in particular, the style of Christianity to which the 'Johannine' writings (John's Gospel, 1, 2, and 3 John, and Revelation) bear witness has marked differences of emphasis from the 'Pauline' Christianity of Paul's authentic letters and of the various works attributed to him, such as the 'Pastoral Epistles' (1 & 2 Timothy and Titus). Some biblical scholars suggest that even the very earliest Christian communities were already sharply divided according to which 'Christianity' they adhered to. Just as in the modern Church, some may have been more interested in mission and outreach (the Pauline approach), others (the Johannines) in the internal life of the Christian group, seen as a safe haven from a wicked world. But even if that is so, there is no reason to think that the New Testament includes books whose content and approach represented the private opinions of a single person or small group – a minority view that most Christians would have scornfully rejected. The extent of the diversity is not that great; each strand represents an important and influential group within the Church.

Again, in the Old Testament it is possible to discern quite sharp differences of view. For example, there is a 'prophetic' (almost Protestant) belief that God is not pleased with the offering of sacrificial victims, but only with social justice (Isaiah 1.10–17, Psalm 40); and on the other hand there is a 'priestly' belief that sacrifice is, pre-eminently, what God requires (Leviticus 16–17). In the form in which we have them, however, most of the books in which these divergent opinions occur have been adjusted or edited to take account of the other view. So the legal codes in the Pentateuch generally warn that sacrifice is not acceptable *on its own* (Leviticus 19), and the prophetic books stress that those who seek to please God by the way they live should also not omit to offer sacrifice (Malachi 2.13–16). The result is a sort of official line which softens the sharpness of the conflicts that there may well have been in ancient Israelite society. This gives us a set of documents which, for all their differences of emphasis, have a certain unity and coherence born of their semi-official status as the sacred texts of a reasonably united religious culture. People in the ancient world knew roughly what Judaism was, and if they came to look at the books Jews revered, they found nothing there that did not fit in with that knowledge. This is far from saying that the Old or the New Testament is a highly unified or consistent document – as I have been stressing, the collections formed too accidentally and casually for that. But it does still make sense to see them as the semi-official, majority literature of an identifiably coherent religious tradition.

Summing up

All this partly explains why, if we compare the biblical books with the literature of other nations (whether ancient or modern) we are struck by how many of the genres common elsewhere are missing from the literature of Israel and the early Church.

Because the Bible is *religious* literature, it contains no

lyric poetry expressing emotions not specifically religious. There are no legal documents, except where these are quoted within larger works, as the 'Book of the Covenant' (Exodus 21–3) is embedded in the story of Moses on Sinai (Exodus 19–40). And there is no drama – Job is more like a drama than anything else in the Old Testament, but it is hard to think of its actually being performed; indeed, there is no evidence at all to suggest that ancient Israel had anything corresponding to drama.

Because the literature comes from essentially a *single* religious tradition, we do not find in it discussions of the merits of competing philosophies of life such as abound in classical literature. Occasionally 'wrong-headed' opinions are summarised in order to be refuted – as when the Psalmist refers to the 'fool', who 'has said in his heart, "There is no God" ' (Psalm 14.1 = 53.1); or when St Paul outlines objections to his own theology which he then goes on to shoot down (see, for example, Romans 2.1–11, 17–24; 1 Corinthians 15.35–41; Galatians 3.1–5; 4.21–31). But we do not find in the Old Testament, for example, the religious literature of worshippers of Baal. We know, from archaeological finds such as the *Ras Shamra* texts from the ancient Syrian city of Ugarit, that such literature existed; but it has not come down to us within the Old Testament.

Finally, because all the biblical literature is *semi-official*, we do not possess any informal documents such as private letters and diaries, or occasional pieces such as sermons, lecture notes, or handbooks for the use of restricted groups (priests, lawyers, scribes).

Everything in the Bible, so far as we can tell, was intended either by its 'authors' (in so far as these were individuals), or at least by the community that transmitted it, to be literature worthy of attention by successive generations, to be read and received by all.

Biblical Genres

If so many types of writing are *not* to be found in Scripture, what is? The variety is much greater than all these cautionary remarks might lead us to think. For although many genres familiar to us do not occur, others which we are unfamiliar with do. At this point it is necessary to consider the two Testaments separately. We begin with the Old Testament, and must mention five different types of material.

Old Testament. More than half of the Old Testament (almost everything from Genesis to Esther) consists of *narrative*. But this is of many different kinds. In a few places it comes close to what we might recognise as history writing or at least chronicle. Thus parts of the books of Kings clearly (and confessedly) rest on archival, chronicle-like material recording the main events of the reigns of various kings: see, for instance, 2 Kings 1.18, 8.23, 10.34, 12.19, 13.8, 13.12, and so on. For the most part, however, even in the books that cover periods known from other ancient sources, the material is closer in style and conception to what we might loosely think of as legend or perhaps 'saga'. This is not to express a particularly adverse judgement on the historical accuracy of the Old Testament historians' accounts, but merely to note that they are not much like (say) the critical history-writing of the Classical Greek historiographers, still less like that of a modern historian.

In many of the stories in Genesis, Exodus, or 1 Samuel we seem to encounter something approaching folk tale, though never in a 'raw' form – always adapted by the author or editor to make it conform to the official religious context in which it is placed. Occasionally we might want to use the word 'myth', perhaps in connection with some of the early chapters of Genesis, pre-eminently the story of creation (Genesis 1 and 2).

At the other end of the spectrum there are narratives that are by no means traditional folk reminiscence, but on the contrary skilful and conscious literary art: narrative fiction, we might even say. This is surely the case with some of the short narrative books, such as Ruth, Jonah, and Esther, or (in the Apocrypha) Tobit and Judith. It may also be the correct way to read the story of Joseph (Genesis 35–50), or of David (most of 2 Samuel). In these places the narrative style approaches that of a novel or at least a *novella*.

It is highly characteristic of the Old Testament that it does not seem to distinguish these different narrative levels.

> The [biblical] story moves back and forwards, quite without embarrasment, between human causation and divine causation, between the statement and description of events in entirely human terms (no doubt with theological aims, purposes, and overtones, but still in entirely human terms) and the statement of events in a fashion utilising express and large-scale divine intervention. The ability to mingle these styles is a mark of the genius of the literature, but it is also a sign that history is not a governing factor in the selection and presentation of material.[2]

In Kings, for example, the writer moves freely between annalistic documents (e.g. 1 Kings 9.15–28) and legends about the lives of Elijah and Elisha (e.g. 2 Kings 1 and 2). Sometimes it appears to record two different versions of the same events, one dry and factual, the other embellished with supernatural interventions. This is perhaps so in the case already mentioned above, the

account of the siege of Jerusalem by the Assyrians in
701 BC (2 Kings 18–19), the source of Byron's poem
'The Assyrian came down like the wolf on the fold'.
The modern reader's sense that a story in which an
angel of the Lord takes a leading role is simply not the
same kind of thing as a story in which human political
decisions lead to political consequences is not shared by
the biblical narrators themselves. This is an important
point which we shall have to return to in discussing the
Bible as history.

Embedded within the narrative framework of the
Pentateuch we find large blocks of material which,
from a Jewish perspective, give it its character as
'Torah' – the *laws* supposed to have been given to
Moses on Sinai. They were either passed on by him to
the people then and there (as recorded in Exodus from
chapter 19 to the end of the book, in virtually the
whole of Leviticus, and in the first half of Numbers – in
effect, the middle of the Pentateuch); or else they were
reserved by him for communication later, at the moment when the Israelites were about to enter the
Promised Land (as recorded in Deuteronomy). As already mentioned, these laws are for the most part in a
form known from other ancient near eastern cultures.
The laws cover a range of topics, from the minutely
detailed ordering of worship to the basic ordinances of
human society. But traditionally the Ten Commandments (or Decalogue), found in Exodus 20 and Deuteronomy 5, are seen as the heart of all the legislation.
Even though 'secular' laws presumably existed, all the
laws in the Pentateuch have been edited to introduce
clear reference to God.

The Book of Psalms contains what may be seen as the
hymnbook of the ancient Israelite temple. The forms
that these hymns or prayers take are in some cases

known from other ancient cultures, though we have no other compendium quite like the Psalter. It is hardly ever possible to say with certainty when individual psalms were written; nor is it known (though there are many theories about it) which of them had a liturgical origin and which were originally religious lyrics for private use. Some may have been first one and then the other, just as today people may use hymns as private prayers or, conversely, may adopt what were originally religious lyric poems as hymns for communal singing. Psalm 25, for example, seems to be an individual's prayer in trouble:

> To thee, O LORD, I lift up my soul.
> O my God, in thee I trust,
>   let me not be put to shame;
>   let not mine enemies exult over me . . .
>
> Be mindful of thy mercy, O LORD,
>   and of thy steadfast love,
>   for they have been from of old.
> Remember not the sins of my youth, or my
>   transgressions;
>   according to thy steadfast love remember me,
>   for thy goodness' sake, O LORD!

Yet the psalm ends, 'Redeem Israel, O God, out of all his troubles' – as though the whole psalm is meant to be read as the lament of Israel personified. It seems likely that this is a case of adapting an individual lyric for corporate use.

Conversely, Psalm 3 came to be used in both Judaism and Christianity as the 'morning' psalm *par excellence*, and was consequently treated as though it were about the trials and the salvation of an individual safely delivered from the night to begin a new day:

> O LORD, how many are my foes!
>   Many are rising against me;
> many are saying of me,
>   there is no help for him in God.
> But thou, O LORD, art a shield about me,
>   my glory, and the lifter of my head.
> I cry aloud to the LORD,
>   and he answers me from his holy hill.
> I lie down and sleep;
>   I wake again; for the LORD sustains me.

But it is fairly clear from a closer examination that the 'I' who speaks is really a personification of the nation, at war with the massed armies of a heathen foe:

> I am not afraid of ten thousands of people
>   who have set themselves against me round about.
> Arise, O LORD!
>   Deliver me, O my God!
> For thou dost smite all my enemies on the cheek,
>   thou dost break the teeth of the wicked.
> Deliverance belongs to the LORD;
>   thy blessing be upon thy people.

Psalms also occur outside the Psalter, embedded (like the laws) within narrative: for example, Exodus 15, 1 Samuel 2, or Jonah 2.

There are many examples in the Old Testament of *proverbs* or aphorisms, constituting what in the study of the ancient Near East is traditionally referred to as 'wisdom' literature – the forerunner of what we should call philosophy. Such literature had its home in the royal court and especially in the schools attached to the court for the training of royal officials. It is found plentifully among the documents discovered in royal palaces both in Egypt and in Mesopotamia. The major biblical

collection of wisdom is the book of Proverbs, but Job
and Ecclesiastes (and Ecclesiasticus in the Apocrypha)
show indebtedness to the same traditions of learning.
How close the Old Testament wisdom writers were to
their foreign counterparts can be seen by comparing
texts from Proverbs with excerpts from *The Teaching of
Amenemopet*, mentioned above, e.g.:

> Do not remove an ancient landmark
>   or enter the fields of the fatherless;
> for their Redeemer is strong;
>   he will plead their cause against you.
>
> (Proverbs 23.10)

> Do not carry off the landmark
>   at the boundaries of the arable land,
> nor disturb the position of the measuring-cord;
> Be not greedy after a cubit of land,
>   nor encroach upon the boundaries of a widow.
>
> (*Amenemopet* 6)

> Better is a little with the fear of the LORD
>   than great treasure and trouble with it.
> Better is a dinner of herbs where love is
>   than a fatted ox and hatred with it.
>
> (Proverbs 15.16–17)

> Better is poverty in the hand of the god
>   Than riches in a storehouse;
> Better is bread, where the heart is happy,
>   Than riches with sorrow. (*Amenemopet* 6)

> Diverse weights are an abomination to the LORD,
>   and false scales are not good. (Proverbs 20.23)

> Do not lean upon the scales nor falsify the weights,
>   Nor damage the fractions of the measure.
>
> (*Amenemopet* 16)[3]

Finally – a form with no real modern parallels – the Old Testament ends with the recorded utterances of *prophets*. The prophets were figures who spoke in times of national crisis, and claimed to reveal the will of God and his intentions for the future good or ill of the nation. Few parts of the Old Testament are superficially so puzzling to the modern reader. The prophetic books consist, for the most part, of quite fragmentary utterances, not necessarily recorded in the order they were delivered. In almost all cases they have been extensively reworked, sometimes over a period of several centuries – first by disciples of the prophet, and then by successive generations of scribes seeking to update the prophet's sayings and make them relevant to ever-changing situations.

New Testament. It is tempting to draw parallels between the Old Testament and the New. Just as the Old Testament contains narrative+wisdom (teaching)+prophecy, so, one might say, the New Testament contains narrative (Gospels and Acts) + teaching (Epistles) + prophecy (Revelation). But the resemblance is rather superficial, and conceals the enormous difference in the genres of writing actually encountered in the New Testament. The New Testament is not simply a set of imitations of the Old Testament Scriptures: it is a product of the richly mixed cultural heritage of the first-century Mediterranean world, called Hellenistic because its common language was Greek, but containing elements from Semitic and Persian as well as Greek culture.

Some parts of the Gospels do seem to be a conscious attempt to provide the Church with a Christian equivalent of the Old Testament. The birth-stories in Matthew and Luke, for instance, look very like the Old Testament accounts of the birth of such heroes as

Samson (compare Judges 13 with Matthew 1–2 and Luke 1–2). The prologue to the Gospel according to John is definitely a Christian 'Genesis' ('In the beginning . . .') But as a whole the Gospels are nothing like any Old Testament narrative books: they belong to the Greek genre of biography or memoir. Paul's Epistles, similarly, resemble nothing in the Old Testament, and indeed are not consciously 'Scripture', but are more like a modern papal encyclical or pastoral letter. And Revelation, though it describes itself as 'the book of this prophecy' (Revelation 22.10), is less like the books of the Old Testament prophets than it is like the genre known as the 'apocalypse' – an account of the coming end of the present world-order, described through weird symbolism apparently seen in a vision. Many examples of this can be found in the literature of the last couple of centuries BC, but only one (partial) example found its way into the Old Testament, the book of Daniel. Rather than being a collection of occasional sayings, like the books of the Old Testament prophets, Revelation is a carefully crafted and coherent work, which sets out a detailed panorama of the end of time.

The New Testament does have examples of one genre embedded in another, just as we have seen to be the case in the Old. Paul occasionally seems to quote hymns which may have existed before him (e.g. Romans 1.3–4; Ephesians 5.14; Philippians 2.5–11; Colossians 1.15–20). It is the sayings of Jesus, now recorded in the Gospels, that are most like the sayings of the prophets, in that they must originally have had an independent existence, being first remembered as isolated units and only later worked into connected narrative frameworks by the evangelists. That this is so, is apparent as soon as we observe that the same saying may occur in a different context in different Gospels.

Conclusion

We have already said that the Bible has a certain 'official' character. This does not just mean that it has been *given* such a status by Judaism or Christianity. In declaring these books to be 'Scripture' both religions were doing little more than recognise the status they *already* had, and which had come to them naturally and uncontroversially. But the variety we have now uncovered is bound to make us ask what it means for such a diverse work to be 'Scripture'. To be bound by a creed, or some other formal definition of faith, may be a problem, but it is plain what it means: a creed says, 'This is what is to be believed', and one can either agree or disagree. But in what sense can one either affirm or deny a collection of narratives, laws, poems, aphorisms, biographies, letters, and visions? In that all these documents come, as we have seen, from a (reasonably) unified religious tradition, it makes some sense to say that those who accept them as 'Scripture' are committed to that tradition. Jews and Christians believe that it is the God to whom the Old Testament bears witness who is the true and living God; Christians add that he is also the God who shines through the biography and the sayings of Jesus, and whom the writers of the Epistles were trying to get their readers to understand and believe in.

But this does not sound very much like the popular picture of what it is for Christians to 'believe in the Bible', with all the commitment that usually implies to the literal, historical truth of its narratives and the absolutely binding character of its laws. It suggests, rather, that the relation between the contents of the Bible, and the religious faith the Bible helps to nourish, is a somewhat oblique relation. From earliest times Christians have found it necessary to adopt formulations of what they believed – such as the creeds – and set these alongside the Scriptures as parallel sources of authority. It is not hard to see why. The Bible is not very well suited to function as a textbook of right belief, and it is probably only by freeing the Bible from the expectation that it can so function, that we become able to hear what it is actually saying.

CHAPTER FOUR

The Bible and the Critics

There is nowadays a 'pluralist' approach to religion in many circles, which has the laudable aim of breaking down the barriers of suspicion between adherents of different religions. It is enshrined in much modern religious education in schools. Although on the positive side it is a powerful weapon against prejudice and for mutual understanding, it does also have its drawbacks. One of these is a tendency to treat all religions as essentially similar branches of the same firm, naturally with different personnel, fixtures, and fittings, but all possessing the basic essential items of equipment without which religion cannot function. Among these, typically, people expect to find: regularly recurring festivals; some sort of clerical or priestly functionaries; distinctive modes of dress, food, and drink; and some 'scriptures'. Thus we ask: if Christians celebrate Christmas, what do Hindus celebrate? If Jews have rabbis, what do Sikhs have? If Muslims read the Qur'an, what do Buddhists read?

There is no denying that a sympathetic 'feel' for religions other than our own can result from this approach. It can remind us just how many structural similarities there are between many of the world's great religions, despite the obvious differences in content. At the same time, we need to be on our guard. Sometimes the bits of equipment one faith possesses have a different order of priority from what look like the corresponding bits in another; and this may indeed be one of the most important contrasts between the two faiths. For example, Catholics have priests and Jews have rabbis - but they do not have the same function in the two religions, and many Jews will be quick to say that the tendency in western countries to treat the rabbinate as a kind of Jewish priesthood is deeply misleading. Conversely, the place of special foods in Judaism is structurally far more significant than in Christianity. The tendency, for example, of Christians to eat chocolate eggs at Easter is quite marginal, as compared with the Jewish insistence on unleavened bread at the Passover meal – not to mention the distinctions between kosher and non-kosher food in general.

Religions of the Book

The status of 'scripture' in various religions is a particularly sensitive example of the importance of not jumping to conclusions through a kind of bland religious tourism. In modern times it has become usual to see the three major monotheistic faiths – Judaism, Christianity, and Islam – as united in being what the Qur'an calls religions 'of the book'. All three accord a place of honour to their (respective) Scriptures. But the place of the Bible in Christianity differs in important ways from that of the Tanak in Judaism or of the Qur'an in Islam – and, indeed, the last two also differ from each other. Islam is perhaps the purest case of a 'religion of the Book' anywhere in the world. The sad affair of Salman Rushdie's *Satanic Verses* has reminded people in the West of just how important the sanctity of the Qur'an is to Muslims. Many Muslims have dissociated themselves firmly from the death-threats to Mr Rushdie from some Shi'ites, but all agree that to speak with disrespect of the Prophet and the holy Qur'an is, for any Muslim, the ultimate blasphemy. The Qur'an is believed to have been literally dictated to Muhammad by God, and it is a central doctrine in Islam that its Arabic style is 'incomparable'. Indeed, it must be read in Arabic, not in translation, since that is the very tongue in which God spoke it. (Translations of the Qur'an are usually not so described, but are referred to as 'paraphrases' – attempts to give the reader some idea of what the Book is about. Strictly speaking, it is impossible and/or illicit to translate the Qur'an.)

Furthermore, it is held that the Qur'an has been miraculously preserved from error: scribes have never falsified the text. Anyone who has ever copied even a short document knows that on every page a few errors will creep in, however careful one tries to be. Of course in modern book-production a whole art of proof-reading has grown up to eliminate such errors, and scribes in the ancient world also knew of techniques to ensure that their mistakes would not 'corrupt' the texts they were copying. But in the case of the Qur'an, it is believed, God himself ensured that there is not a single case where chance errors have resulted in mistakes in the text. The Qur'an is thus in every way a perfect, and perfectly divine, document.

The Hebrew Bible is not seen in quite this way in Judaism, though it is central to the mainstream of Jewish tradition to think of it as divinely given. Very great care is taken in the copying of books, especially of the books of the Torah, but it is not usually said that divine providence enters into this process. Rather, scribes have to take precautions precisely because, being human, they could make mistakes and so endanger the accurate transmission of the text. And the centrality of the Torah is rather differently conceived in Judaism from the usual Islamic view of the Qur'an. It is freely acknowledged that Judaism is a developing phenomenon. It must always remain rooted in Scripture, but successive generations of authoritative interpreters of this Scripture share in the authority of the text they interpret. Scripture is thus a dynamic, growing phenomenon, not a static entity given once for all at the beginning; 'Torah' means the Pentateuch, or sometimes the whole Bible, but it also means the accumulated decisions of rabbinic authorities in expounding the scriptural text. Nevertheless, most varieties of Judaism can reasonably be described as book-centred. In some kinds of Jewish mysticism, in fact, the Book becomes almost more important than the world: the whole created universe is felt somehow mystically to belong inside the Torah, which existed before the world was created and which will go on existing after the world has ended. It is a kind of transcript of the mind of God himself, and studying it is the highest possible form of wisdom for human beings.

There are undoubtedly forms of Christianity which are close to Jewish or even Islamic attitudes towards Scripture. A chorus which I remember singing as a child began 'Cling to the Bible, though all else be taken!' I can remember asking myself even then, '*All* else? The church, the sacraments, prayer, human affection?' But certainly there are Christians who would say so, and a high regard for the power and authority of the Bible is undoubtedly an option within the spectrum of Christian belief. In Christian churches of every kind the Bible has, of course, a special place. Public readings from it are often begun or ended by a reminder to the hearers that what they are receiving is the word of God, not merely a human communication. People meet in small groups to study the Bible, they read a chapter or more a day as part of their religious discipline, and (as we have already noted) they often expect a Bible to look different from any ordinary book. In all these ways the Christian Bible can be seen as Torah-like or Qur'an-like in its centrality to the Christian faith.

Yet it is also clear that most Christians do not feel quite the same kind of reverence for the Bible as Muslims feel for the Qur'an or Jews for the Torah. Christianity has traditionally possessed, alongside the Scriptures, more or less formal definitions of the essential core of the faith. These may take the form of creeds – used in nearly all Christian traditions; in Protestant Churches, 'confessions' – such as the Augsburg Confession, a basic document for Lutherans, or the Westminster Confession, fundamental to the Reformed Churches in Britain, especially the Church of Scotland; and in Catholicism the decisions of Church Councils, together with papal decrees and encyclicals.

In Protestantism it has been customary to argue that any such document must be congruent with Scripture: that is, it may not require anyone to believe doctrines that cannot be demonstrated from Scripture. But this has never meant that such documents were therefore deemed unnecessary. Very firmly Protestant organisations, such as the student Christian Unions, never regard it as sufficient for members to declare their allegiance to the Bible; they have a short checklist of essential doctrines which the would-be member must sign. Furthermore, Christians of every persuasion will maintain that what God has revealed *through* Scripture, namely his gift of himself in Jesus Christ, is logically prior to Scripture itself – even though they may at once go on to say that we would not know of it without Scripture, and that what Scripture tells us about it is wholly without error.

What we see in all this is a sense that while the Bible may well be perfect and irreplaceable, yet the religion to which it bears witness is not quite a religion 'of the book' in the Islamic sense. Christians, however Bible-centred, are sensitive to any charge that they *worship* the Bible. Furthermore, they will always stress that the Bible was given through human agents. In modern times at least Protestant defenders of scriptural authority have usually been at pains to stress that they do not think the books of the Bible were actually dictated by God (as the Qur'an allegedly was to Muhammad). They have agreed that the different style and genre of different books (described in the previous chapter) demonstrate just how firmly God's self-revelation was anchored in the very human conditions of particular historical settings, in ancient Israel and in the early Church. All this would be freely conceded even by those who most staunchly defend the divine authority of Scripture. Christians of a more 'liberal' cast of mind would naturally go much further still in emphasising the human element in the Bible. And they would point out, with justice, that the greatest Christian interpreters of Scripture (such as St Augustine or John Calvin) have always treated the books as individual works by particular people who wrote from a specific situation. If the Bible is nevertheless to be seen as 'divine', that will be because God has the power to turn the works of the human intellect into vehicles for his own self-communication – not because the Bible is really a document he wrote himself and miraculously 'planted' in the world.

Thus the idea that each book of the Bible should be studied in its own right, and not treated merely as a random slice of a homogeneous holy book, is not a product of modern scepticism. It has always been built into Christian thinking about Scripture to a far greater extent than is the case in Islam or even Judaism. Christian faith and the Holy Bible are not identical: there is a logical space between them. Christians may believe that the authors of the biblical books are the ultimate and authoritative interpreters of the faith, but even then they will see them as real people, not simply human word processors printing out a text whose writer is God.

Biblical Criticism

The attempt to do justice to this conviction that the books of the Bible express the thoughts of real, specific authors, who had ideas they were trying to express, is what is meant by 'biblical criticism'. The word 'criticism' naturally sounds warning bells in the minds of some Christians: who are we, they ask, to 'criticise' the Bible? But it is meant neutrally, rather as in 'literary criticism', which means the application of rigorous thought to the assessment of literary works, not necessarily the expression of adverse judgements on them. A biblical critic is someone who tries to discover what the biblical authors were really saying, against the background of their own time and in their own terms. Being critical about the Bible is not the opposite of being in favour of it – very few people would bother with biblical criticism if they did not think that the Bible was a book of major importance, well worth spending immense amounts of energy on. Being critical is the opposite of being uncritical. An uncritical approach to Scripture means finding in it only what we expect to find – whether because we already 'know' (from church tradition, from our own prejudice, or from the assumptions within our culture) what it will contain, or because we are not prepared to make the effort to grapple with the sometimes difficult ideas the biblical writers use. Biblical criticism means an attempt to hear the text speak, rather than being at the mercy of its interpreters whether ancient or modern.

It is true that biblical criticism as an organised enterprise is a product of the post-medieval world. Even though its roots go back into the earliest Christian times, it became a major force only from the Renaissance onwards, and made its greatest advances in the nineteenth century. Two factors have been especially important in producing what we now know as biblical criticism.

One factor is Protestantism. This would be rather paradoxical, if biblical criticism meant a negative attitude towards the Bible; for it was Protestantism that restored the Bible to a positive place in the Christian scheme of things. It is precisely the close connection of biblical criticism with Protestantism that helps to show how far biblical criticism is from implying a negative approach to Scripture. One essential conviction of the sixteenth-century Protestant Reformers was that the traditions of the church ought to stand under the authority of the Bible, and to be corrected, if necessary, in the light of what the Bible said. But what did the Bible say? As the Reformers saw it, the medieval church had very neatly ensured that its teachings would never be corrected in the light of the Bible, because it had included among those teachings the principle that the meaning of the Bible could be determined only by interpreters authorised by the church. The result was a perfectly closed circle: the Bible had authority over the church, but the church alone had power to determine what the Bible meant. This built-in institutional safeguard against being challenged by one's own foundation document is, indeed, highly characteristic not only of religions of the book but of other organisations for whom a fixed text is crucially important. Where a written text is in theory the final arbiter, any decision has to be defended as if it were a conclusion drawn from this

65

authoritative document. Human nature being what it is, the document then tends to be interpreted rather 'creatively' so as to support the decision one wishes to reach anyway.

The Reformers argued that the church typically went against the 'plain sense' of the Bible in certain of its teachings, and that reform would come about only if people began to read the Bible without the filter of traditional teachings to come between themselves and the text. The logic of this is that one should approach the text while leaving on one side the question whether or not it will turn out to conform with traditional teaching; and then worry afterwards about whether traditional teaching may need some adjustment. In that sense, biblical criticism is not only not opposed to Protestantism, it is a child of the Protestant spirit.

The second factor in the rise of biblical criticism is the renewed curiosity in the beginnings of things which surfaced in Europe with the Renaissance – thus at around the same time as the Reformation. The origins of the Bible became as interesting as the origins of the Classical cultures of Greece and Rome, which were being rediscovered in the fifteenth and sixteenth centuries. The first manifestation of this in the realm of biblical studies can be seen in the rise of a serious *textual criticism* of the Bible. Textual criticism is the art of reconstructing the correct wording of texts – that is, the wording as it left the hands of the original author or first scribe. This reconstruction works by discovering and eliminating the errors which successive generations of scribes inevitably introduce. A pioneer in the textual criticism of the New Testament was Erasmus (*c.* 1466–1536), who began a tradition of recovering the original text by collating and comparing all the available ancient manuscripts, using logical deduction to establish, in places where there are variants, which of the various 'readings' must be the oldest.

But before long a concern for the exact text opened up wider questions as well. What if a scribe had artificially joined together two originally separate texts? This might also be discovered, by analysing discrepancies or contradictions in a biblical book. How was the phenomenon of the Synoptic Gospels to be explained – that is, how does it happen that Matthew, Mark, and Luke often preserve verbally identical versions of the sayings or actions of Jesus, and yet in other ways tell a slightly different story? Who copied from whom, or did all three have access to one or more older documents? These more speculative questions, sometimes called 'higher' criticism to distinguish them from the 'lower' (i.e. more basic) task of textual criticism proper, began to grow in importance in the seventeenth and eighteenth centuries. In England an alliance began to be formed between the asking of such critical questions and a certain detachment towards the claims of the Christian religion, and many of those who took an interest in biblical criticism were freethinkers such as Thomas Hobbes (1588–1679). It is from this time that the suspicion of biblical criticism by orthodox Christians really derives.

In the nineteenth century Germany became the chief centre of biblical criticism, which linked hands once more with the Protestant concern for reading the Bible on its own terms. The result of this marriage between an essentially rational biblical criticism and the Protestant defence of the Bible against church tradition has resulted in a strong emphasis, in all the Reformation Churches, on training clergy and ministers in the skills of biblical criticism. Even here however, just as much as in traditional Catholicism, there has been a tendency for this to lapse in pastoral practice. The great nineteenth-century German liberal theologian, Adolf von Harnack, once remarked: 'I bleach my students with historical criticism as much as I can, but once ordained they all gradually discolour again.'

Biblical criticism is thus, in principle, an attempt to establish the *publicly available* meaning of the biblical texts, the sense that they have for readers who have not already made up their minds what they can be allowed to mean. At least until recently, it was taken for granted that such criticism must in some sense be 'historical' (as in the remark just quoted from Harnack). This does not mean that criticism has been concerned only with history, in the sense of historical events, but that it has operated with the assumption that what a text means depends on when and by whom it was written: that its meaning has a certain historical rootedness. After all, even the meaning of words changes over time. To read any text, you need some idea of the state of the language at the time it was written. But it is also important to know what kind of text you are reading – what genre it belongs to; for if you read a poem as though it were a piece of prose, you are likely to make silly mistakes in understanding it, just as you will misread a legend if you understand it to be a newspaper report. This means that biblical critics have to discover what types of writing actually existed in the world of ancient Israel and in the early church – some of the examples given in the previous chapter were the fruits of such enquiries. Clearly, too, it will make a difference to the meaning of a text if parts of it were composed at a later time than other parts; so the *unity* of texts has to be investigated. All these questions form part of the agenda for biblical criticism. The overall aim is to discover what the various books of the Bible mean; but along the way many complex questions about their origins, date of composition, authorship, and unity have also to be asked. Not surprisingly, seeing how difficult such questions are, many biblical critics have spent so much time on them that they have never proceeded to the question of meaning – sometimes giving the impression that ultimate questions about the meaning and truth of the Bible do not interest them. But in fact the enterprise of biblical criticism as a whole *is* directed to establishing the meaning of the text, however many interesting byways it sometimes allows itself to be diverted into.

Some of the practical conclusions reached by biblical critics formed the basis for my account of the contents of the Bible in the last chapter. A particular concern has long been the relative dates of different biblical books. For example, most critics now hold that Mark is the oldest of the Gospels, not Matthew as was long thought; that Paul's epistles are all older than the Gospels; that the Pentateuch is the result of weaving together four originally separate works, dating respectively from the ninth, eighth, seventh, and fifth centuries BC, and that the latest of these 'sources' postdates the work of the great prophets such as Isaiah and Amos. These datings may sound dry, but their cumulative effect produces a very different impression of the development of ancient Israel and the early church from that held by most 'innocent' readers of the Bible.

A further important contribution of biblical criticism has been the avoidance of anachronism in reading the Bible. Critics try to be aware of, and allow for, their own prejudices. No one can do this with complete success, but criticism involves a sustained effort to come as near to it as possible. Biblical writers must be understood as much as possible within their own context. This is a difficult task when reading any literature from the past, but when texts have been read and re-read as often as the Bible, and continue to be religiously important for people today, it is especially hard to block out later applications of the text and to read it on its own merits. In reading Paul's epistles, for example, it is vital to see that they are addressed to a quite specific situation in one or other of the churches in the first generation of Christians. Paul was not writing in the first instance for 'us'. As we progress in a critical reading of biblical texts, we become aware that the thought-world from which they come is remote from our own; and the task of appropriating and applying the text in our own context becomes harder though also, perhaps, more rewarding.

I have tried to present biblical criticism as its practitioners see it. But although for more than a century now most people engaged in Christian ministry in the mainstream churches have had at least some training in criticism, many in the churches perceive it negatively, as undermining the Christian faith. Furthermore, very few people outside the theological world are more than dimly aware of the main conclusions the critics have come to. Indeed, even from pulpits one hears little about the results of biblical criticism – in this Harnack's dictum remains all too true.

Biblical criticism in its beginnings was a child of intellectual curiosity, and of the Protestant willingness to challenge accepted ideas and institutions on the basis of a free reading of the Bible. The problem, for those who are trying to exercise authority in the churches, is that once you allow such freedom, there is no knowing where it may lead. Once historical questions are asked about the Bible, they can only be given historical – which means in principle undogmatic and revisable – answers. Biblical criticism begins with the desire to have firm ground under our feet by a return to the Bible; it ends by showing us that all ground is shifting, because a fresh discovery, a new theory, can undermine what we thought was certain. There are many signs that the churches are not happy to live with 'criticism', that is, with open and unrestricted enquiry, but prefer tradition, uncritically accepted.

At the same time, there have been some victories for the critics. Much of the impetus for ecumenical reform has come from those who have come to see how insecure is the basis of much that divides the churches. This is so, for example, in the spheres of ministry and sacraments, where a critical reading of the relevant biblical texts in their historical context effectively wipes out the impression that the New Testament church had fixed and unalterable 'orders' of ministry, or an agreed sacramental theology. At the same time, critics have also shown how important, for Paul in particular, was the unity which Christians should share, and to what an extent it was meant to break down rather than reinforce existing barriers – for example, between Jews and Gentiles within the Christian community, between slaves and free men, between women and men.

The fact that the ground rules for effective biblical criticism are not dependent on denominational allegiances, but only on sound reasoning, means that for practical purposes the religious commitment of critics is entirely irrelevant to evaluating their work. Consequently, biblical criticism is engaged in by Christians and Jews, by Catholics and Protestants, by believers and non-believers, and all belong to a common community of scholarship which is independent of any of the churches. It is understandable that this should cause anxiety to those whose main task is to maintain the independent structures of Christian denominations. At the same time, it is noticeable that biblical criticism has so far been remarkably unsuccessful in causing churches to modify any of their agreed doctrines or dogmas. Its success has lain only in getting them to see that these dogmas are not so absolute as they once seemed. A Christian community that actually took as its starting-point what can be known from the Bible, read critically, rather than what has traditionally been taught in the church, slightly modified in the light of criticism, is as far away as ever it was. It would be an interesting phenomenon if it ever came about.

CHAPTER FIVE

The Bible as History

The Bible as History[4] was the title of a popular book of the 1950s, by the Swiss writer and journalist Werner Keller. Keller sought to demonstrate that a multitude of stories in the Bible (especially in the Old Testament), which modern sceptics typically dismissed as legend or myth, could be shown from archaeological evidence to be grounded in historical reality. Examples were the Flood, the destruction of the walls of Jericho in the time of Joshua, and the conditions in Israel in the days of the great prophets. Much more revealing than the English title is the original German, *Und die Bibel hat doch recht!*, 'So the Bible is right after all'. Keller's book was warmly welcomed by Christians who felt that the tendency of modern biblical criticism had been to throw doubt on the Bible's reliability. They drew the encouraging message that Christian confidence in the church's foundation document was fully justified. Modern scientific archaeology, so far from challenging the biblical record, vindicated it at every turn.

Why Try to Prove that the Bible is Historical?

What motivation is there for an approach such as Keller's? Two are possible, one religious and the other not. On religious grounds one may think it vital that the Bible's version of historical events is accurate, because this reflects on its reliability in general. Few people would suppose that every historical detail recorded in the Bible has a religious significance in itself. For example, Jericho is said (in the book of Joshua) to have been captured by the incoming Israelites through a semi-miraculous collapse of the walls, so that the invaders were able to capture it without needing to fight (see Jos. 6), but other cities are recorded as being taken after a long and bloody battle (see, for example, Jos. 8.18–29 and 11.1–15). The conquest of Palestine thus took place, according to the Bible, by a mixture of normal military tactics and divine intervention. Now it is presumably not a detail that matters from a religious point of view whether Jericho was captured in one way and Hazor in the other, rather than the other way around. If one is anxious that the biblical record should be accurate, that is not because the content of each recorded incident is *in itself* significant. It is that the accuracy or otherwise affects one's overall confidence in the Bible. If the Bible could get one or more incidents significantly wrong then, it is argued, we have no reason to trust it in general, and this has a knock-on effect on all other biblical stories. If the Bible misreports the conquest of Jericho, why should it not misreport the resurrection of Jesus? The religious reason for being glad that 'archaeology vindicates the Book of books' (the subtitle of Keller's work) is that it removes us from the top of a slippery slope, down which significant inaccuracies at any point in the biblical record threaten to propel us, ending up with complete scepticism about everything reported in the Bible.

A second, non-religious concern should also be noted here. Keller drew on some of the interpretations of archaeological digs by the American school of archaeologists founded by W.F. Albright (1891–1971), a key figure in biblical studies throughout the middle part of this century. Though willing to concede inaccuracies in the biblical record, Albright tended on the whole to argue that his archaeological discoveries vindicated it. His arguments were humanistic rather than religious and appealed to common sense against too much intellectual refinement. Albright was confronted with a school of thought characteristic of German biblical studies between the wars, in which the biblical record was allowed only a very subordinate place in the reconstruction of events and conditions in ancient Israel. Archaeological data were being assessed without regard to any light the text might throw upon them and then, as often as not, used to reconstruct a course of events strongly at variance with the story the Bible tells. Against this Albright staunchly defended the biblical chroniclers, arguing that more often than not a painstaking search of archaeological data showed that they were essentially reliable, even if occasionally wrong on points of detail. His basic principle was that we should operate with an attitude of charity towards the Bible, rather than always looking askance at the story it told. If we did that, then we should see that the Bible was usually uncannily accurate. Why should we assume, perversely, that people who were far nearer than we are to the events they recorded always blundered, or even wilfully misrepresented the facts? Trust the biblical writers, and you will find that they seldom lead you astray! – such was the Albright school's motto.

A rather similar attitude can be seen in recent Israeli archaeology, some of which has been directed by experienced military commanders. They have frequently argued that biblical accounts of battles may look exaggerated or implausible to desk-bound western scholars; but anyone who has fought over the same terrain can vouch for their intimate knowledge of conditions on the ground. The book of Joshua, they say, is as good as a military manual. Both here and in the

Albright school's approach there may be a measure of religious motivation, connected with a commitment to the Bible as Holy Scripture. But much more evident is a respect for the biblical text simply as an ancient document all too easily dismissed by over-clever modern Westerners. Give the Bible a chance, they say, and it will surprise you.

We should note that such approaches to 'the Bible as history' are essentially *rational*. They do not say: the Bible is divinely inspired, *therefore* all that the Bible says is true – regardless of what 'secular' evidence may suggest. Such a position can of course be maintained. We may simply take the Bible as a given, and then argue that any apparently contradictory evidence from other sources must necessarily be false. For example, some Christians have reacted in this way to scientific evidence suggesting that the world is older than implied by the chronological scheme in the Bible. (According to the Bible, the world is now about 6,000 years old.) The Bible is right, such Christians have said; so you must be misinterpreting your data, because to leave the biblical account out of the reckoning is to disregard the most important piece of evidence there is or ever can be. But this is *not* the line of thought pursued by Keller or by adherents to the Albright school of 'biblical archaeology'. For them, the validity of modern scientific or archaeological methods is not in doubt. What they argue is that *as a matter of fact* the conclusions to which archaeological study leads turn out to conform with at least the underlying sense of the biblical record, not to contradict it. The Bible is not assumed to be right, as a matter of principle; but it turns out to be right 'after all'.

The strength of this approach is that it is open to the evidence, to follow wherever it leads. But for the Christian who wants to be sure of the reliability of the Bible, that is surely also its weakness. The accuracy of the biblical record can never then be any more certain than the conclusions of science or of archaeology, and these (as scientists and archaeologists will be the first to remind us) are never more than the best available hypotheses. They are always corrigible in the light of fresh evidence. There are many examples of such correction in the history of archaeology in biblical lands. The walls of Jericho are a case in point. In 1930–6 John Garstang claimed to have discovered in his excavations decisive corroboration for the story in Joshua 6. The walls of Jericho certainly had been destroyed, and in his opinion the date fitted well the period of the Israelite conquest of Palestine. Of course this did not show that the walls had collapsed through direct divine action; but it did lessen people's scepticism about the story, by showing that a sudden and dramatic collapse had occurred. Keller, in his first edition, made a good deal of this 'vindication' of the biblical narrative. Unfortunately, subsequent excavation by Kathleen Kenyon revealed that the destruction of the walls had occurred in the Early Bronze Age, probably around 1900 BC – on any plausible dating, some 600 years at least before the exodus. The period when the Israelites must have been moving in to settle in the Promised Land, on the other hand, has left no evidence at Jericho. In the Late Bronze Age (c.1200 BC) there was no fortified wall at Jericho at all, and there are no signs of any dramatic change in the inhabitants, so far as this can be established from artefactual evidence. There are many other examples of the failure of archaeology to confirm details of the biblical record, just as there are others where it does confirm them. The important point to grasp is that good archaeologists do not work either to confirm or to contradict the biblical or any other traditional account, but to establish the facts. Whether the facts are palatable to religious believers or not does not, strictly speaking, lie within the archaeologist's terms of reference. Those who are believers themselves may hope that their findings will fit the biblical account; but any attempt to doctor these findings is simply dishonest archaeology, and no reputable archaeologist will have anything to do with it.

It seems to me that we must give up *either* the assured reliability of the Bible, *or* our willingness to follow where the evidence leads: we cannot have both. The impression that we can is to be obtained only by highlighting the places where, as a matter of fact, the biblical record *is* substantially borne out by archaeological evidence and keeping quiet about those where it is not, and this is not a very honest way of proceeding. I am not trying to convince the reader that the Bible is hopelessly unreliable at every point – that would be merely to fall into the opposite error! How accurate the Bible is should be regarded as a genuinely open question.

In What Sense is the Bible Reliable?

The issue that this then raises is as follows: is there a degree of unreliability beyond which we ought to say that the Bible is 'discredited', and consquently that any religious faith that takes its stand on the Bible should be abandoned? It will be clear that I do not think such a point has been reached the moment one can show that there is some inaccuracy in the Bible – that is to make a higher claim for the Bible than is necessary. But suppose, for the sake of argument, it could be shown that every major event recorded in the Bible failed to happen – difficult to imagine, but let us suppose it. Not only did the walls of Jericho not fall down when the people shouted, there never were any Israelites at Jericho anyway, or Jericho never even existed; there was no exodus, no settlement of the Israelites in Palestine, no exile; Jesus never existed; the story of the church in Acts is a complete fabrication from start to finish; and the letters of Paul are all forgeries from centuries after the period they purport to be addressed to. Would that matter?

Surely it would. However much Keller overplayed his hand in *The Bible as History*, he correctly perceived that it does matter whether the Bible gives us a *substantially* accurate impression of the events it describes or is, on the contrary, thoroughly misleading. Honest people will not go on calling themselves Christians if they become convinced that there is no God. Similarly, we should distance ourselves from the Christian faith if we come to think that the story of Jesus is a pure fabrication, and that no such person ever lived, died, or rose again. Christians differ, as a matter of fact, about where one should draw the line in all this. 'Conservative' Christians would be distinctly unhappy if it could be shown, for example, that Abraham or Moses never existed (of course, it is not clear how this negative judgement ever could be proved). More 'liberal' believers will usually be happy to think that the stories about these men illustrate important truths about God and his relationship with his people, whether they actually existed or not. But very few Christians indeed believe that the line cannot be drawn somewhere. In this sense virtually all Christians think of the Bible as containing at least some accurate historical information, and hold it to be vital that it does so.

Now we can ask the essential question this discussion has been leading up to. *Why* does it matter whether or not there is accurate historical information in the Bible, at least about certain central events? We have already answered the question by saying: 'central' events. For Christians it is a matter of great moment that Jesus of Nazareth actually lived, and that the picture of him we get from the Gospels is substantially reliable – that he is not simply a character in a story, however good a story, but a person who actually existed in human history. But from this point other historical consequences radiate. For Jesus belongs in a particular history, the history of Israel; and he is bound himself to have had some clear impressions about that history – impressions drawn at least partly from the Old Testament. So that history, too, needs to be more than a fiction or a dream. It follows that Christians cannot lightly contemplate a completely non-historical Bible, but are committed to some core of fact within it.

However, to approach the matter from this end is to see it very differently from *The Bible as History*. From the present perspective, we could perhaps say that most such attempts to 'vindicate' the Bible – whether from archaeology, science, or historical study – invert the proper order in which the historical nature of the bibli-cal account matters. One gets the impression from Kel-ler's book, and also from much that is written and spoken in opposition to what people call the 'scepti-cism' of biblical criticism, that what matters most is the reliability of the Bible. If we can prove, say, that the walls of Jericho did fall down, or that Jesus really was tried before Pontius Pilate, that helps to vindicate the Bible, and so makes its divine inspiration and authority credible. But this is to look through the wrong end of the telescope. The central events of the gospel matter for Christians in themselves. They would matter whether or not they appeared in the Bible. The very earliest Christian communities believed in the life, death, and resurrection of Jesus, but they did not read about these events in a gospel, because no gospels had yet been written: the evangelists belonged to the second and third generations of Christians. To put the matter in a deliberately exaggerated way: Jesus did not rise from the dead to confirm the reliability of the gospels! The events in which Christians believe are logically prior to the book which records them; and the question how accurately the Bible does record them is not crucial because it affects the status and authority of the Bible, as an end in itself. It is crucial because (since we *happen* to have virtually no historical sources besides what is in the Bible) it determines whether we actually possess any real knowledge of these events.

This point is sometimes made by saying that the Bible matters as a *witness* to the events Christians regard as central, or that the Bible is our primary *evidence* for what Christians believe: it is not itself the *object* of that belief. Here there is a considerable difference from some other book-centred religions. For Judaism, we could fairly say that the Moses of the Bible is more important than the 'real' Moses – if indeed we could ever establish what he was like anyway. There are also Christians for whom the Jesus of the New Testament similarly seems more important than the real historical person, Jesus of Nazareth. But most Christians, faced with such a stark choice, would deny this, and say that the New Testament account is only an access route to take us to Jesus, and is not itself the goal we set before us. For practical purposes there is no need to set the person against the book; but in principle the person has the priority.

So we are to treat the biblical texts as routes by which to approach the central historical events on which Christian faith rests, rather than being primarily interested in the reliability of these sources in themselves. How can this be done in practice? In principle the Bible should be subjected to just the same methods of historical enquiry as any other document from which we hope to reconstruct past events. For the last 150 years, biblical critics have tried to do precisely that. Sometimes their more 'negative' conclusions strike some Christians as unduly sceptical; but historical investigation must be allowed to follow the truth, and not undercut by a 'hidden agenda', in the form of a desire to be 'orthodox', if the evidence points in an 'unorthodox' direction.

It is commonly said that ordinary believers are upset and disturbed by critics, who seem to be telling them that there are things in the Bible which are untrue. Even if it is true that some Christians find the suggestion of 'untruth' in the Bible scandalous, I think it is worth remembering that for many people it comes on the contrary as a surprise to learn that the Bible is in fact of any historical value at all. People tend in our culture to adopt an all-or-nothing attitude towards the Bible (see chapter 1). So it is widely assumed that Christians are obliged to believe every historical affirmation in the Bible. Because this would entail believing some things that ordinary people rightly regard as incredible (Adam and Eve, a total world flood), non-Christians generally assume that therefore *nothing* in the Bible is worth believing. But I believe many Christians are just as deeply sceptical about the Bible's historical truth as their non-Christian friends. They 'believe' it in a special sense which removes it from the real historical world, and are quite surprised when one speaks of events recorded in the Bible in the same breath as events of 'secular' history. For example, the straightforward question, 'Did Moses live just before or just after Tutankhamun?' will produce much the kind of blank reaction that one would get if one asked 'Did Little Red Riding Hood live before or after George III?' People, that is to say, accept the truth of the Bible – perhaps even of the whole Bible, including the parts that really are *not* history – when functioning in their 'faith' mode, but seldom really treat it as historically important in the same way as 'secular' or 'real' history. Dorothy L. Sayers caught the atmosphere of this kind of thinking admirably:

> Most children, I suppose, begin by keeping different bits of history in watertight compartments, of which 'Bible' is the tightest and most impenetrable. But some people seem never to grow out of this habit . . .
> Cyrus was pigeonholed in my mind with the Greeks and Romans . . . And then, one day, I realised with a shock as of sacrilege, that on that famous expedition he had marched clean out of Herodotus and into the Bible.

The reference here is to the Persian king Cyrus's campaign against Babylon in about 538 BC, when the Babylonian empire fell to his forces almost without resistance. Cyrus is mentioned in the book of Isaiah (44.28 and 45.1), and his decision to let the Jewish exiles return to Palestine is described in Ezra 1.1–4. Sayers goes on to describe the shock when she discovered that the king in the book of Esther is also a figure known from 'secular' history:

> . . . King Ahasuerus. A good Old-Testament-sounding name, Ahasuerus, reminding one of Ahab and Ahaz and Ahaziah. I cannot remember in what out-of-the-way primer of general knowledge I came across the astonishing equation, thrown out casually in a passing phrase, 'Ahasuerus (or Xerxes)'! Xerxes! But one knew all about Xerxes. He was not just 'classics', but real history; it was against Xerxes that the Greeks made their desperate and heroic stand at Thermopylae.[5]

It is a pity that Sayers took Esther as her example, since it is probably the clearest case of complete and intentional fiction in the Bible! However, her point is a good one. On one level, ordinary Christian believers probably assent to more of the historical narratives in the Bible than most scholars: one can feel a chill run through the congregation if one suggests from a pulpit that stories in the gospels, for example, may have been made up. But on another level many believers fail to connect the truth of the Bible with other kinds of truth, and so are genuinely surprised to learn that there is 'straightforward' historical truth in its pages.

Where should the historian studying the Bible begin? The first task is to decide which parts of the Bible are *capable* of yielding any real historical information. In a sense any text reveals something about 'history', but it may be only the history of the time when it was written. It is only in this sense that one obtains 'historical' data, for example, from the Books of Chronicles, or from the 'tales' such as Esther, Ruth, and Tobit. These works are not 'historical' in the sense that they record history. Chronicles is an imaginatively rewritten version of Samuel and Kings, retelling the events as they *should* have happened. The other books mentioned are fiction, and were intended to be read as fiction. We can, however, learn from them how people saw the past in the centuries when these books were written, and the very anachronisms in such texts are revealing. For example, Chronicles has Hezekiah send invitations to a great festival by the royal mail (2 Chronicles 30.1–12). This is a highly unlikely institution for Judah in the eighth century, but easily thinkable for a Jewish writer of the fourth century (which is probably when Chronicles was written), who was familiar with the Persian royal messenger service.

But many biblical texts really do rest on a basis of good historical information. This is pre-eminently the case with the Books of Kings, which contain extracts from contemporary royal annals, identified as 'the book of the chronicles of the kings of Judah/Israel' (not to be confused with the biblical books of Chronicles). In the New Testament, which will perhaps interest Christians more, most scholars are agreed that Acts shows a detailed knowledge of customs and institutions in the Roman world which should lead us to treat the story it tells very seriously as historical narrative. This is not to say that we cannot question it. All too often it is clear that the author has an axe to grind, and he is no neutral, scientific historian – no biblical writer is that. The author of Acts, for example, has an interest in portraying the institutions of the Roman Empire as on the whole benign and positive, whereas Judaism emerges in very dark colours. But Acts is not a fairy tale, any more than the Gospels. To return to the comments made in earlier chapters about the genre of the Gospels: these works are biographies, not legends. They may be inaccurate or misleading. Indeed, from the discrepancies between them, it is plain that not everything in all of them can be true. Jesus may have cleansed the Temple at the beginning of his ministry (John 2.13–22) or at the end (Matthew 21.12–13, Mark 11.15–17, Luke 19.45–46); but whichever of these possibilities is correct, the other must be wrong – unless we say that he did it twice, which means that *all four* Gospels are wrong, since they all imply that it was a single incident. But the Gospels are the kind of narrative that is *capable* of being true or false, unlike imaginative fiction, folklore, or myth. They are written 'from faith to faith', not to provide historians with interesting information but to convert doubters to faith in Jesus and to sustain believers in their faith. Yet the vehicle they use for this task is one that a historian can assess critically. The Gospels are vulnerable to historical enquiry. That is part of the historical rootedness of Christianity, which is not a general 'philosophy of life', but makes specific historical claims which can at least in part be tested for plausibility.

This does not mean that it is easy to decide what in the Gospels is directly historical, and what owes something to the imagination of the later generations of Christians who put these books together. Some things in the gospel story, most notably of course Jesus' resurrection, are necessarily beyond the reach of direct historical investigation. We can say for certain that many people believed Jesus had risen from the dead:

> I delivered to you as of first importance what I also received, that Christ died for our sins in accordance with the scriptures, that he was buried, that he was raised on the third day in accordance with the scriptures, and that he appeared to Cephas [=Peter], then to the twelve. Then he appeared to more than five hundred brethren at one time, most of whom are still alive, though some have fallen asleep. Then he appeared to James, then to all the apostles. Last of all, as to one untimely born, he appeared also to me. (1 Corinthians 15.3–8)

Similarly, we can note that the Gospels record people finding the tomb empty (Matthew 28.6; Mark 16.6; Luke 24.3; John 20.2,5). We can argue that without a firm conviction that Jesus was alive again, the early church would soon have lost heart. But this is not to say that there is historical proof for the resurrection. It is false to say, as people sometimes do, that biblical critics assume 'resurrection' to be impossible and so seek other explanations. Biblical criticism, like all serious historical enquiry, can deal only with the sorts of historical event to which there are parallels; before an allegedly unique event, such as the resurrection of Jesus, it is simply dumb. Leaving out of account the central mystery of the Christian faith should not therefore be taken for scepticism.

For the most part, however, historical work on the Gospels is able to treat the material as we should treat the ingredients of any other biography, ancient or modern. It is essential to ask from what raw materials the narratives were put together, who wrote them, how long after the events this happened, and what aims the authors may have had in view that could have distorted or coloured their presentation. In principle we could ask the same of Boswell's *Life of Johnson*. But two factors add to both the fascination and the difficulty of this task where the Gospels are concerned.

First, there is the strange fact that we have not one but four Gospels. Furthermore, these are not four totally divergent accounts of the life of Jesus, but represent two main streams of thought. Matthew, Mark, and Luke tell recognisably the same story, even though with many differences of emphasis. But until we reach the story of Jesus' trial and execution, John's Gospel could almost be about a different person, for there are scarcely any incidents in common with the other three, 'synoptic' Gospels. We have already mentioned the story of the 'cleansing of the Temple', where there is a straight conflict between the Johannine and the synoptic account. It might be added that John's Jesus speaks in a quite different style from the Synoptics' Jesus – in sustained discourses, many of them about himself, rather than in parables and pithy sayings.

Since the early years of the Church there have been many attempts to 'harmonise' the Gospels, and one early Christian teacher, Tatian, produced a book called the *Diatessaron* which is a complete harmony, and which was used for several centuries in the Syriac-speaking churches of the Middle East. But it is clear that the Gospels really tell significantly different stories. Even among the Synoptic Gospels there are major differences. The Christmas story as popularly known is an amalgam of the different accounts in Matthew and Luke. Matthew gives no hint of the adoration of the shepherds, Luke seems unaware of the 'wise men'. And Mark has no birth story at all; nor has John. At the same time, at least among the Synoptic Gospels it is clear that there must be some literary relationship. Most modern scholars think that Mark's is the oldest account, and that Matthew and Luke knew and used Mark in more or less the form we now have it: this is the only explanation of the frequently identical wording. Matthew and Luke may well have shared some other source or sources in common. Each of them seems also to have known traditions about Jesus that were unknown to the other (as in the birth narratives just mentioned). Of couse they may have made some of their material up, or at least changed it to fit the story they were telling.

It would be pleasant to report agreement on these matters among scholars, but this is far from being the case. We may feel tempted to say that since the scholars cannot agree, it would be far safer just to believe what the Gospels say. But this should be resisted; to believe 'exactly what the Gospels say' is to believe four incompatible accounts of Jesus' life, death, and resurrection. The price we have to pay for believing some parts of the story to be wholly true is to accept that other parts are false. There is little sign that the churches as a whole have ever grasped this nettle, but they should. The uncertainties of all scholarly reconstructions of the life of

Jesus are obvious; but attempts to harmonise the four Gospels are just as speculative. Of course we may want to argue that the discrepancies do not seriously matter for faith. But that, even if true, is the answer to a different question. The form of the Gospels as we have received them means that as soon as we ask the question 'What, in detail, actually happened?', we are forced either into scholarly enquiry or into harmonisation. The former is at least subject to rational control; harmonisation is little more than the free play of the imagination.

Secondly, as soon as we study the Gospels in detail and note both the resemblances and the disagreements between them, we begin to see that not only the cleansing of the Temple, but many other incidents too, occur in rather different places in the story told in each individual Gospel. There can be little doubt, for example, that the story of the miraculous catch of fish in Luke (5.1–11) and in John (21.1–8) is the same story, but in one Gospel it occurs during Jesus' early days in Galilee, in the other after his resurrection. Not much ingenuity is needed to guess that the Gospels are to some extent arrangements of anecdotes about Jesus, made at a time when the exact date and place of each had been more or less forgotten. Some stories dated themselves, especially those that could only have taken place during Jesus' last days in Jerusalem, but many others could have happened at almost any point during his work in Galilee or his journey to Jerusalem. The evangelists, like any biographer faced with undated fragments, did their best, but they were not infallible. And often, indeed, it is not clear that the exact dating matters much anyway. Most people thinking back over their own lives find it difficult to date many events relative to each other. On turning out old photos or diaries they may be quite surprised to find that two incidents remembered as quite separate actually happened on successive days, while others which had been remembered together because of some sort of 'thematic' resemblance were in fact separated by several years. The 'profile' of Jesus which the Gospels build up is more important than the exact chronology. Indeed, it could be argued that by refusing to reduce the Gospels to a single, harmonised account the church (perhaps unwittingly) more or less forced us to see Jesus through a somewhat soft focus. Perhaps it thus directed our attention away from exact biography and towards an engagement with the whole shape of his character and purpose. The fact remains, however, that for the historian the essentially anecdotal character of much in the Gospels makes writing a 'life of Jesus' virtually impossible.

Conclusion: What kind of Bible have we got?

At the risk of appearing to make a virtue of necessity, we might find food for thought here. Christians sometimes take it as read that God will have wanted to provide us with a perfect, wholly reliable account of what Jesus did and said. On the basis of that assumption they then harmonise furiously until the Gospels seem to provide what is required. A more sober procedure is to ask what, in fact, the Gospels are like. From that it follows that if God gave us these books, then either he tried to provide a perfect account but failed, or that was not his intention anyway. The question is not what kind of Bible we think we ought to have, but what kind of Bible we have got. The Bible we have got is manifestly not a perfect historical record. But that may remind us of something that in any other sphere than religion we should take for granted: that the very idea of a perfectly accurate historical record of anything is a will o' the wisp. Any record written in human words is going to be partial, conditioned by the culture from which it comes, and incomplete. A total record of everything that happens even in a single minute is simply a logical impossibility – what do we mean by 'everything'? For religious purposes what matters is that the Bible should be sufficient, not that it should be perfect; and this the Christian faith has consistently judged it to be. For the uncommitted historian, what matters is that it should be interesting, and should stimulate open-minded historical enquiry. Few texts have been so successful in doing so.

CHAPTER SIX

Biblical Morality

'Wanted: A Return to the Ten Commandments!' said a large poster I spotted outside a church in West London. It captured a feeling shared by many people today, that society would be altogether better if we returned to this traditional source of western morality. The feeling is as common among non-Christians as among believers, for it is the ethical standards above all that people tend to admire in the Christian tradition, even if they do not accept its religious teachings. Often, indeed, they wish that the ethics could be detached from the supernatural or 'mythical' claims which Christians have insisted on linking with them. A common complaint against the churches today is that their interest in all kinds of abstract speculations about God and Jesus (not to mention the nature of Christian ministry) has deflected Christians from their primary task. That task is to defend and exemplify the basic standards of moral decency which the Ten Commandments stand for. 'Back to the Commandments!' would be a popular rallying cry well beyond the boundaries of the church.

The Ten Commandments (sometimes also called the 'Decalogue') occur in two places in the Old Testament: first at Exodus 20, where they are given to the people of Israel at Mount Sinai; and again in Deuteronomy 5, where Moses repeats them to the people (with a few variations in detail) just before they enter the Promised Land. Rather surprisingly, they are not referred to anywhere else in the Old Testament, though it is possible that Hosea 4.2 and Jeremiah 7.9 allude to them. By New Testament times, however, they were definitely regarded as an essential summary of the ethical demands of the Jewish religion, as can be seen from Matthew 19.16–22 (and its parallels in the other Synoptic Gospels, Mark 10.17–22 and Luke 18.18–23), the story of the rich man who asked Jesus what he must do to obtain eternal life. Jesus' reply reminds him of the core of the Commandments: 'You shall not kill, You shall not commit adultery, You shall not steal, You shall not bear false witness, Honour your father and your mother', though adding also 'You shall love your neighbour as yourself' from Leviticus 19.18.

Traditionally the Commandments are thought of as divided into two 'tables' (according to Exodus 32.15 the Commandments were written on two tablets), concerning duties to God and duties to one's fellow human beings. Jesus' own 'summary of the Law' (see Mark 12.28–34) draws out the essentials of each 'table' in a still terser form by linking the verse from Leviticus with the great summary of Jewish faith from Deuteronomy 6.4–5: 'Hear, O Israel: The Lord our God is one Lord; and you shall love the Lord your God with all your heart, and with all your soul, and with all your might.' Love of God and of our neighbour are thus seen as the two essential themes of Jewish – and Christian – ethics, taught respectively in the first four and the last six of the Commandments. In the seventeenth and eighteenth centuries it was common in England to place the text of the Commandments in churches, usually directly above the altar. Along with the Apostles' Creed and the Lord's Prayer, also treated in this way, they were thus held up to everyone as the heart of the Christian religion.

Now it is possible, by taking the call 'back to the

Commandments' very literally, to show that they are not quite such a useful basic moral code as people often think. First, the predominant tone is negative. Apart from 'Honour your father and your mother', the Commandments all forbid wrongdoing, rather than commending virtue. Most of them could be kept by staying in bed all day and avoiding any human contact. Secondly, and more importantly, they envisage a very specific form of human society which is by no means the kind we live in, and are evidently addressed only to certain people within that society. The person addressed in the Decalogue has a wife, a house, cattle, servants, and parents; he (definitely he) can give orders to others about resting on the sabbath, and he is competent to give evidence in court. He is, in fact, a free adult male householder – the only kind of person who enjoyed full legal rights in ancient Israel, and who also bore full responsibility for the ordering and defence of villages, towns, or cities. The society of the Decalogue is one in which elderly parents surrendered their independent status in return for the protection and support of their adult sons, in which wives, children, and slaves had a lower legal (not necessarily social) status, and in which the entire economy depended on the efforts of smallholders, who jointly made up the council which directed the affairs of each local community.

This is the society of roughly the tenth to the seventh centuries BC. In the time of Moses (in, perhaps, the thirteenth century) it quite certainly did not yet exist. If we think that Moses really gave the people the Decalogue in the wilderness, we shall have to believe he was giving them a code that had little bearing on life as they were then living it, and which would come into its own only much later – after settlement in the Promised Land and the beginning of settled agricultural life.

Equally, after the exile in Babylon in the sixth century BC Jewish life in Palestine and in the communities of the Dispersion was no longer the life of a predominantly rural people, nor had most Jews any stake in organising the life of the pagan towns and cities where they lived as aliens. Indeed, the pattern was already breaking up well before the exile, when the inhabitants of Jerusalem, Samaria, and some other great cities already exhibited some of the rootlessness of many urban societies. They certainly did not consist of smallholders with a few cattle and some fields. If we had to guess at the time when the Decalogue was formulated, we might fix on the ninth or eighth centuries BC; though of course there is no reason why individual Commandments may not have been older than this, and nor can we rule out the possibility that they were added to afterwards.

The text of the Commandments is quite untidy. The length of the individual Commandments varies greatly; some have explanatory notes and others do not; and it is strange to find, among prohibitions of definite and specific wrong *actions*, what seems to be an attempt to legislate against wrong *thoughts* ('Thou shalt not covet'). It is not even clear exactly how the text should be divided to yield the traditional ten 'words'. Catholics and Protestants, for example, have disagreed about whether 'I am the LORD your God' and 'You shall have no other gods but me' are two Commandments or two parts of the first Commandment, and this then has consequences for the identification of the third Commandment. But whatever the exact truth may be, it is clear that the Commandments are not the text we should produce if we were trying to provide a summary of ethics for our society. Like everything in the Bible, they are the product of particular circumstances and conditions. So we might say: if you really want to 'get back to the

Commandments', then you must realise that this means a fundamental reordering of society; not just in terms of its moral tone, but in terms of its basic structures. Alongside honouring God and our parents we shall need to have slavery and the subordination of women; alongside respect for property and marriage, fierce sabbatarianism and a compulsory 'extended family' system. Some may think all this quite desirable, but it is not, surely, what most people mean when they speak of a return to the Ten Commandments.

From the Commandments to Christian Ethics

Of course such close attention to the exact kind of society envisaged in the Commandments is not what we have in mind if we take them as somehow typical of 'biblical morality'. I have set out the problems rather starkly because there is, in some currents of thinking in the Church today, an almost fundamentalist zeal for the Commandments; and I think it is important to be clear that this, if encouraged, could have unexpectedly unpleasant consequences. But most people think of the Decalogue in the spirit of Jesus' summary of the Law: love and respect for our fellow men and women, and for the God who made both them and us, as the basis for living life as it is meant to be lived. Accordingly what people have always done is to generalise from the Commandments; to infer (positive) duties from the (negative) prohibitions; and to detach the substance of the Commandments from their anchorage in a particular, now obsolete form of society. Let us take each of these in turn.

First, generalisation. If adultery is wrong, then it can be reasoned that other irregular forms of sexual conduct should also be forbidden. It is difficult to get people to agree about which. Ancient Israelite society certainly generalised in this way, developing a very complex code

of sexual morality (see, for example, Leviticus 20) –
though some of the conclusions it drew do not now
commend themselves to either Christians or Jews. For
example, there are no laws against polygamy or prostitution in the Old Testament, while on the other hand
homosexual practices are punished by death. Again, if
murder is wrong, then we may well argue that all mani-
festations of unreasonable anger and violence – of
which murder is only the extreme form – are also to be
condemned (Exodus 21.18–27). And if theft is a sin,
then attempted theft or even the excessive desire for
someone else's property, which can issue in theft, must
be seen as wicked. In this last case, as we have seen, the
Decalogue itself makes the transition: the last Commandment condemns 'coveting' other people's possessions (Exodus 20.17, Deuteronomy 5.21).

The Old Testament is full of examples that show how
positive obligations can be generated from the prohibitions in the Decalogue. If people are to live in a society
where murder, theft, and adultery should not occur,
then they need to practise the virtues of respect for
human life, honesty in all their dealings, and loyalty to
the ties that bind them to their spouses and families.
Much of the book of Proverbs consists of admonitions
whose purpose is to achieve this sort of society:

Do not say to your neighbour, 'Go, and come again;
tomorrow I will give it' – when you have it with you.
Do not plan evil against your neighbour who dwells
trustingly beside you. Do not contend with a man for
no reason, when he has done you no harm. Do not
envy a man of violence and do not choose any of his
ways; for the perverse man is an abomination to the
LORD, but the upright are in his confidence (Proverbs 3.28–32).

In this, the Old Testament is part of a general tradition in the thought world of the ancient Near East. All the ancient societies we know, in Egypt, Mesopotamia, or Asia Minor, shared a considerable body of ethical teaching and agreed on the importance of fostering peace, honesty, stable family life, justice, and harmony between all. They also agreed that it was the special duty of kings and rulers not only to ensure that the law was justly administered and wrongdoers punished, but also to take care of the needs of those in no position to protect or help themselves – typically 'widows and orphans'. You have only to look at the monuments produced by kings in the ancient world (for example, by the particularly brutal Assyrian rulers of the ninth and eighth centuries BC) to see that in their dealings with conquered enemies they were capable of extreme violence and oppression. But in ruling their own subjects they were heirs to a long moral tradition which insisted that the test of a good king was his care for those with no one to defend them. Biblical morality inherits traditions of social justice and honesty which had a long pedigree in the ancient world – not found in the moral teachings of all human cultures, but ubiquitous in the Middle East.

Thirdly, the drive to produce from the Commandments a universal ethic which is not attached to any particular type of society was already an important element in Judaism before the time of Jesus. Especially among the Jewish intelligentsia in Egypt, in and around Alexandria, attempts were made to show that Jewish morality contained all that was best in the moral traditions of mankind. All could benefit by modelling their lives on the patterns revealed to Moses. A difficulty here was caused by the detailed *ritual* regulations of the Old Testament. Writers such as Philo (born in about 20 BC) gave them rather implausible allegorical interpretations, but the central moral tenets of the Decalogue were not hard to commend to interested inquirers. Many Greeks and Romans were attracted by the purity of the Jewish ethical system (though repelled by such features as circumcision and the kosher laws).

The teaching of Jesus, as recorded in the Syneptic Gospels, belongs in this tradition of appealing to what is universal in Jewish morality. Plainly for Jesus the moral teaching of the Ten Commandments was basic. As we have already seen, it lies at the heart of his own 'summary' of the law. But at the same time he often expounds moral principles by an appeal to what is true for all mankind, not just for the Jews. 'Love your enemies and pray for those who persecute you, so that you may be sons of your Father who is in heaven; for he makes his sun rise on the evil and on the good, and sends rain on the just and on the unjust' (Matthew 5.44–5). Where the Torah is actually tightened up – as in Jesus' severe teaching about divorce (Mark 10.2–9) – it is by appealing back to principles inherent in creation which can correct the permissions given by Moses at a much later time: 'From the beginning of creation "God made them male and female". "For this reason a man shall leave his father and mother and be joined to his wife . . . What therefore God has joined together, let not man put asunder." ' Christianity dealt with the problem of the ritual and purity laws of the Jews, which did not appeal to non-Jews, by the simple but drastic means of simply declaring that they were now abrogated. Stories were told of how Jesus himself had declared them to be no longer operative in the new order - see, for example, Mark 7.14–23.

Most forms of Judaism have never acquiesced in the way Christians relativise the 'ceremonial' laws. Jews have rejected the implicit contrast between 'morality' on the one hand and 'mere ritual' on the other. But Christianity from earliest times has regarded the distinction as important. In Christian discussion of the place of the Old Testament, it has been usual to distinguish between the moral laws which are valid for all times and cultures – and of these the Ten Commandments are the supreme example – and the ritual legislation, which was applicable only for Judaism and only for the time before the coming of Christ. In modern times there has been a greater willingness among Christians to learn from Judaism, and students of the Bible have come to see that even if Christians are not 'bound' by the ritual laws, these do express important insights into the proper relationship between humanity and the created order. With recent concern for ecology comes a realisation that cultures and religions which ritualise behaviour connected with food, the natural cycle, and the daily round may have something to teach those which are more focused on human relationships. No doubt Christians are 'free' from the obligation, for example, to avoid certain foods as 'unclean' (Acts 10). But if this 'freedom' leads to an exploitative attitude towards the natural order, it is freedom at the expense of the rest of God's creation. It is a sound principle of biblical morality that one's own freedom must not be at the expense of others. Christian disregard for the 'ritual' laws may thus in some ways have been too cavalier, too much concerned only with behaviour towards other *people*. We now see that our relationship with the natural world also has a moral dimension, and of that such things as food laws may at least be a potent symbol, even if we do not take them literally.

Once we allow for these various ways of moving from the particularity of the Ten Commandments (and of other expressions of 'biblical morality') into something more universal, we can see the call 'back to the Commandments' is not as simplistic as it might at first seem. There is a recognisable 'style' of ethics in the Bible: a concern with justice, respect for life and property, honesty and loyalty in sexual and social relations, and positive concern for all that is helpless – whether people with no one to look after them, or the natural world which is at the mercy of human beings. A society in which everyone lived by the ethics of the Bible would on the whole be healthier than the one we live in. That said, there remain two problem areas in thinking about ethics in the Bible.

The Old and the New

Most people take it for granted that there is an enormous contrast between the moral teachings of the Old and the New Testament. So far I have presented 'biblical morality' as if it were an undifferentiated whole. But surely the New Testament itself speaks as though its own moral system were infinitely superior to that of the Old? 'You have heard that it was said, "An eye for an eye and a tooth for a tooth." But I say to you, Do not resist one who is evil. But if anyone strikes you on the right cheek, turn to him the other also' (Matthew 5.38–9). The Old Testament is generally understood as teaching implacable vengeance – both as a desirable goal for human beings to pursue in their dealings with each other, and as the way God himself acts towards them. Whereas in the New Testament we learn to forgive our enemies, and to believe in a God who (in a passage already quoted) 'makes his sun rise on the evil and on the good, and sends rain on the just and on the unjust' (Matthew 5.45).

There is some truth in this contrast. Forgiving one's enemies has never been a central tenet of Jewish belief (though magnanimity and justice certainly have been), whereas it has been quite central to Christian thinking – in theory: Jews might with good reason remind Christians of the other gospel-saying, 'By their fruits you shall know them.' The theory is seldom matched by the practice. But to present the Old Testament as concerned with revenge and the new with forgiveness is a gross oversimplification. The principle, 'An eye for an eye and a tooth for a tooth' (Exodus 21.24, Leviticus 24.20, and Deuteronomy 19.21) was originally intended to regulate revenge, and to bring it under the control of an equitable law. It is a very early statement of a basic principle of justice and fairness, and it contrasts with a primitive desire to annihilate one's enemy and everything belonging to him, and also with the kind of all-too-sophisticated legal systems of many other ancient Near Eastern cultures. In most of these the penalty for a crime depended not on the severity of the injury but on the relative status of the offender and the victim. In Babylonia a slave would die for a minor injury to a nobleman, but a nobleman would pay only a trivial fine for killing a slave. The *lex talionis*, as the 'eye for an eye' principle is known after its Roman equivalent, is crude; but it does express a basic sense that law should set limits to both human blood-lust and human arbitrariness. What Jesus condemns is the attitude that makes this originally limiting principle into a pretext for just the vengeful spirit it was meant to exclude.

The New Testament, it must be said, does not always live up to Jesus' own teachings. Both in Acts and in Paul's epistles we find plenty of instances of a desire for vengeance (for example, Acts 5.1–11, 12.20–3; Galatians 5.12; 2 Thessalonians 1.5–10). The God who strikes down Ananias and Sapphira for their deceit, to the satisfaction of Peter, seems fairly remote from the

God of the Sermon on the Mount. And remote from the God of at least some books of the Old Testament. Deuteronomy, for example, continually stresses the *love* of God for his people, and his unremitting desire to forgive their sins, as does the prophet Hosea:

'I will heal their faithlessness;
I will love them freely,
for my anger has turned away from them.'

(Hosea 14.4)

So far as relations between human beings are concerned, the Old Testament like the New has much to say about respect for shared humanity, which transcends personal enmities and differences of status or nationality.

If you meet your enemy's ox or his ass going astray, you shall bring it back to him. If you see the ass of one who hates you lying under its burden, you shall refrain from leaving him with it, you shall help him to lift it up. (Exodus 23.4–5)

The stranger who sojourns with you shall be to you as the native among you, and you shall love him as yourself. (Leviticus 19.34)

'If I have rejected the cause of my male or female slave, when they brought a complaint against me; what then shall I do when God rises up? When he makes inquiry, what shall I answer him? Did not he who made me in the womb make them? And did not the same God fashion us in the womb?' (Job 31.13–15, my translation)

But the Old Testament does contain certain specific commandments, attributed to God, which cannot be squared with these general moral precepts. Such com-

103

mandments nearly all occur in the context of the Israelite conquest of the Promised Land, and it is they that
are largely the cause of the bad name the Old Testament has acquired for brutality and bloodthirstiness.
From the time of Moses onwards it is made clear that
the Israelites are to take over the land of Palestine from
its native Canaanite inhabitants not peacefully but by
extreme violence. They are by no means to use the
minimum necessary force, but on the contrary they are
to destroy every living being in the land:

> When the LORD your God brings you into the land
> which you are entering to take possession of it, and
> clears away many nations before you, the Hittites, the
> Girgashites, the Amorites, the Canaanites, the
> Perizzites, the Hivites, and the Jebusites, seven
> nations greater and mightier than yourselves, and
> when the LORD your God gives them over to you,
> and you defeat them; then you must utterly destroy
> them; you shall make no covenant with them, and
> show no mercy to them. (Deuteronomy 7.1–2)

Failures to carry out this command meet with bloody
retribution from God. Indeed, as late as the time of the
Hebrew monarchy (in the eleventh or tenth century
BC) it is said that Saul's fall from divine favour resulted
from his failure to put a conquered king and his people
to the 'ban' (*herem*), as it is known (see 1 Samuel 15;
compare Joshua 6.17–21).

Admittedly, this command to wipe out the native inhabitants does not recur in later ages. For example,
after the exile, when a new settlement of the land was
eagerly looked for and in part achieved, we hear nothing
of any desire to achieve this by military means (not that
it would have been feasible anyway). The old 'holy war'
directives are spiritualised into a challenge to be re-

ligiously pure, and to avoid 'mixed marriages' and the like. Indeed, in Deuteronomy, which is full of the language of 'holy war', this process may already have begun. Passages like the one just quoted may reflect less the genuine spirit of the conquest period than the thinking of an age when holy war had already become a symbol of religious reformation, rather than a prescription for actual blood-letting. However, the stories and the laws remain, and are a continuing scandal to most modern readers of the Bible.

From the perspective of any religious conviction that can be held with integrity today, it is hard to see how we can do other than disown these parts of the Bible. Certainly they are a warning against any theory of biblical authority in which all parts of Scripture are to be held in equal honour and regarded as equally binding. Historically, we can try to understand the extreme intolerance of early Israelite religion and its drive to wage a holy war on practitioners of the heathen religion of Canaan. We could say that it was a necessary stage on the route to the pure monotheism that now characterises Judaism, Christianity, and Islam. Monotheism can *survive* without intolerance, though it often does so uneasily. But maybe it would never have *arisen* except out of a religious tradition that had passed through an aggressively intolerant phase. It is open to the reader to decide that the game is not worth the candle. If we can have monotheism only at the cost of the lives lost through the 'holy' wars of the early Israelites then, it may be said, we had better do without it. Perhaps I can sweeten the pill slightly by saying that ancient Israelite historians were notorious for exaggerating their country's military prowess. Modern scholars generally think the Israelite occupation of Canaan was largely peaceful. Huge amounts of Canaanite culture were assimilated, and very few great battles were fought. Holy war is more an ideology than a reality. Nevertheless, one life lost in such wars is one death too many, and the Old Testament narratives are not pure fiction. Most Christian churches read only very sparingly from the 'holy war' sections of the Old Testament (especially Joshua) in their religious services; and this is surely right. At Easter Christians traditionally read the account of the miraculous crossing of the Red Sea, in which 'the waters returned and covered the chariots and the horsemen and all the host of Pharaoh that had followed them into the sea . . . and Israel saw the Egyptians dead upon the seashore' (Exodus 14.28–30). But 'spiritualisation' has done its work here. Scarcely anyone thinks of 'the Egyptians' here as anything but a symbol of all that opposes God. Even so, we might do well in reading this passage to recall an ancient Jewish tradition. When the Egyptians died in the sea, the angels in heaven began to rejoice; but God said, 'My people are drowning in the sea; and you rejoice?'

Law or Gospel?

The other problem about biblical morality is this. In Britain it is common to assume that the Bible is indeed primarily a book about ethics: teaching about how to live a good life, about what it is that God requires of us. Hence a call for the church or the nation to return to the Bible is, like the more specific call 'Back to the Commandments', at least partly a demand for stricter and more traditional moral standards. This is quite close to the traditional Jewish understanding of the function of Scripture as Torah, which was discussed in chapter 2.

One major Christian tradition, however, the Lutheran, is very unhappy about understanding the Bible in this way. According to Lutherans, the Bible contains two elements: 'law' and 'gospel'. The 'law' is not to be equated with the Old Testament nor the 'gospel' with the New (or with the Gospels as individual books). Both are present, intermingled, throughout both Testaments. All of what we have been calling the ethical materials in the Bible have the nature of 'law'. In them we learn what God demands of humanity, what we could do that would please him. So far, so good, it may seem. But (Lutherans add) it is a cardinal error to think that the primary task of the Christian is to ensure that as many people as possible obey the law, so as to build a better and brighter world. As St Paul saw more clearly than anyone, God's demands in fact *exceed* what human beings can possibly fulfil. Although certain basic moral principles are indeed taught in the Bible, and should of course be kept so far as possible, in its entirety the moral system of the Bible has the function of convincing us that we cannot please and satisfy God by our own efforts, however well-intentioned. The law is presented to us chiefly to reveal our own need of God, rather than so that we should erect a system of ethics on the basis of the Bible's teaching. The purpose of this, however, is not to reduce us to despair; quite the opposite. For alongside the law stands the gospel, the 'good news' that God through Christ accepts and forgives us, and is prepared to reward us *as though* we had accomplished the impossible, and kept his Law perfectly.

> There is now therefore no condemnation for those who are in Christ Jesus. For the law of the Spirit of life in Christ Jesus has set me free from the law of sin and death. For God has done what the law, weakened by the flesh, could not do (Romans 8.1–3).

Never, under any circumstances, must the law be

preached without this gospel message of God's free grace to accompany it.

Thus, for a Lutheran, appeals to people to 'return to biblical morality' should be looked at askance by thinking Christians. Naturally, there is no doubt that society would be better if people kept the moral code in Scripture. But there is equally, on the Lutheran view, no doubt that this is an unattainable goal if pursued through human willpower. And Christianity is not primarily a moral system. It is a proclamation of salvation and forgiveness to those who cannot live by a moral system even if they try, not the banal message that God helps those who help themselves.

Other Christian communions have not developed this understanding of what the Bible is for with the same consistency of purpose as the Lutheran churches. Both Catholicism and the Reformed (Calvinist) tradition are more accustomed to say that although much divine help is needed to keep the law of God, and mankind always falls short of it, yet the moral teaching in the Bible was given in order that we might obey it; and there is considerable point in trying to persuade people to 'do as the Bible says'.

Pure Lutheran teaching is rarely encountered in Britain, where none of the mainstream denominations is Lutheran. Those in the Church of England who stress their Protestant, Reformation inheritance tend to look more to Calvin than to Luther for their inspiration, and the English Free Churches derive from various forms of English dissent but owe little to continental Lutheranism. The Church of Scotland is a Calvinist Church, though (like the Church of England) broad in its sympathy towards other traditions. I believe that Lutheran unease about seeing the Bible as a book of morality should be taken more seriously than it is in this country.

The risk in this is that the church appears to abdicate its role as moral critic and moral instructor of society – a role which many in the church regard as exceptionally important. The gain, however, is that the church does not forget that it is itself a collection of fallible human beings, no better than their non-religious contemporaries, who do not deserve the love of God and yet claim to have experienced it in their lives.

Much depends on how one assesses the needs both of the church and of society. My own conviction is that moralism (and with it self-satisfaction) is always a lurking danger for the churches in Britain, and that their constant seeking of a 'prophetic' role, in which they are entitled to lecture everyone else, all too easily hides from them their own internal inadequacies. And at the same time it can deflect them from their first responsibility, to preach not 'law' but 'gospel' to an often deeply despairing society – a society which needs to be shown what God's power and love can achieve, rather than what his justice and law demand. My preferred placard would read 'Wanted: A Return to the Good News': and it would face into the church, not out from it. But that is a theme for another occasion.

CHAPTER SEVEN

A Political Gospel?

In the autumn of 1990, as war in the Gulf began to seem inevitable, David L. Edwards wrote in the *Church Times*:

> In these weeks before war (as it feels), I have been pondering the Old Testament. That is a library full of moral thought about aggression originating in Nineveh, which is near Mosul, and Babylon, which is near Baghdad. The evil of the Assyrian and Babylonian empires is expounded in images which burn the mind. And the disaster inflicted by it on the northern state of Israel proves irreversible.
>
> Yet the prophets are almost incredibly courageous in saying that not all the right is on the side of the Hebrews. For Isaiah and Jeremiah (and others), the invader is the rod which Yahweh wields in anger against the sins of the people whom he loves most. Their own nation's repentance is far more important and hopeful than the formation of any alliance. Isaiah promises that Jerusalem will be spared because Yahweh is still patient. Jeremiah has no such hope. But out of the agonies of these prophets, whose hearts and minds were torn by terrible events, came some of the most sublime visions of a new order. We shall repeat these visions in church at Christmas.
>
> When Christmas comes, will the prophecies be read out as if they concerned solely our religious salvation? . . . Will the Bible be thought to be silent about international politics?

The invasion and destruction of the northern kingdom
of Israel, whose capital was Samaria, in 722 BC can be
traced in 2 Kings 17. The destruction of the smaller
southern sister-state, Judah, by the Babylonians in 587
BC, is described in 2 Kings 23–5. The passages Edwards means us to think about in the prophetic books
are Isaiah 1–11 and Jeremiah 1–45:

> Ah, Assyria, the rod of my anger,
>   the staff of my fury!
> Against a godless nation I send him,
>   and against the people of my wrath I command
>   him,
> to take the spoil and seize plunder,
>   and to tread them down like the mire of the streets.
> (Isaiah 10.5–6)

> Therefore thus says the LORD of hosts: Because you
> have not obeyed my words, behold, I will send for all
> the tribes of the north, says the LORD, and for
> Nebuchadrezzar the king of Babylon, my servant,
> and I will bring them against this land and its inhabi-
> tants, and against all these nations round about; I will
> utterly destroy them, and make them a horror, a hiss-
> ing, and an everlasting reproach. (Jeremiah 25.8–9)

Edwards draws attention to the so-called 'messianic'
prophecies, which early Christians understood to refer
to the coming of Christ and which therefore are still
read at Christmas, especially at carol services –
passages such as Isaiah 9.2–7 ('The people that walked
in darkness have seen a great light . . .') and 11.1–9
('There shall come forth a shoot from the stump of
Jesse . . .'). In their original context, he is suggesting,
these passages were not meant as long-term predictions of the Messiah. Still less were they meant to

concern the 'religious' salvation of individuals. They were political predictions, for which the prophets claimed divine inspiration. They referred to a time, not too long ahead, when universal peace would reign in the world and Israel, purged of its wickedness by military defeat and terrible suffering, would enjoy a new world order in which freedom and justice had replaced war and enslavement. No one can understand these prophetic texts without grasping the essentially political concerns the prophets had. Trying to do so makes the texts bland and colourless, and turns them into nothing more than pretty words for contented and well-fed Christians to enjoy at self-indulgent, cheerful carol services.

An incident on an altogether smaller scale raises similar questions about the political character of the Bible. Early in 1990, the Inner London Education Authority was abolished, and control of schools in Inner London passed into the hands of local authorities. A service was held in St Paul's Cathedral on 28 March to mark the end of ILEA. In designing the service, it was thought that an appropriate reading would be Luke 2.41–52. This records how Jesus, as a boy, stayed in the Temple after his parents had left Jerusalem (where they had been celebrating the Passover). He was eventually found arguing with the most learned teachers of the Jewish law, discussing complex questions on equal terms. This was (I suppose) appropriate as being almost the only passage in the New Testament about 'education' – though it shows that Jesus did not need to be educated, and was therefore perhaps a less than ideal choice. In any case, it was never read. Neil Fletcher, the Chairman of ILEA, when it was time for him to read the lesson, substituted a selection of verses from Isaiah, as follows:

Woe to those who decree iniquitous decrees,
  and the writers who keep writing oppression,
to turn aside the needy from justice
  and to rob the poor of my people of their right.

Woe to you, destroyer,
  who yourself have not been destroyed;
you treacherous one,
  with whom none has dealt treacherously!

The righteous man perishes,
  and no one lays it to heart;
devout men are taken away,
  while no one understands. (Isaiah 10.1–2; 33.1;
                57.1)

This was intended, and understood, as a protest against the decisions of the government, especially those that had led to the winding-up of ILEA. The substitution caused a minor storm. Some argued that it was just what the government deserved and that it had given a cutting edge to an otherwise complacent and bland service; others protested that a church service was not the place to make this kind of protest, that it was discourteous to the cathedral authorities, and that it was a misuse of the Bible for political ends.

It is not my purpose to pass judgement on this incident; clearly there were issues in it that went well beyond the matter of how the Bible is to be understood. But, like David Edwards's piece, it reminds us that the Bible does contain overtly political comments, on almost any conceivable definition of 'politics'. The Old Testament prophets spoke to the political situation of their day not as secular commentators or advisers, but as the mouthpiece of the God of Israel. Their message cannot be *reduced* to a political one, as though the references to the will of God were mere decoration adorning sayings that proceeded from their own political shrewdness and insight. The prophets of Israel were lineal descendants not of the 'wise men' of the ancient world – political advisers, civil servants, scribes – but of inspired ecstatics, such as the people described in 1 Samuel 10.5: 'a band of prophets coming down from the high place [sanctuary] with harp, tambourine, flute, and lyre before them, prophesying'. Their divine call meant everything to them. Yet the message they felt compelled to utter was a deeply political one, that is, it concerned how the nation should be governed, what its foreign policy should be, and what would happen to it when the major foreign power of the day (Assyria or Babylonia) invaded.

The prophets' 'religious' utterances have a 'cash value' in political terms. Their fulfilment is not to be found in the life of the individual Christian today, but in the course of the international politics of the ancient world. At least, this is the primary kind of fulfilment the prophets expected their words to have. Both Jews and Christians have often maintained that hidden within these religio-political pronouncements there was a more secret message for much later generations: either for the generation which would see the advent of the Messiah (now in the past according to Christians, but still in the future from a Jewish perspective) or, more generally, for every generation and for every individual person's relationship with God. Nevertheless, the primary meaning ought not to be ignored, and that meaning very obviously does concern the national and political life of Israel, and the international politics of the ancient Middle East. Here are two further examples:

> Thus says the LORD to his anointed, to Cyrus,
>> whose right hand I have grasped,
> to subdue nations before him
>> and ungird the loins of kings,
> to open doors before him
>> that gates may not be closed:
> 'I will go before you
>> and level the mountains.' (Isaiah 45.1–2)

In this oracle an anonymous prophet of the sixth century BC predicts the conquests of the Persian king, Cyrus (see chapter 5 above), whose victories put an end to the power of Babylon and enabled the Jews to return home from exile.

> Woe to him who builds his house by unrighteousness,
>> and his upper rooms by injustice,
> who makes his neighbour serve him for nothing,
>> and does not give him his wages;
> who says, 'I will build myself a great house
>> with spacious upper rooms,'
> and cuts out windows for it,
>> panelling it with cedar,
>> and painting it with vermilion.
> Do you think you are a king
>> because you compete in cedar?
> Did not your father eat and drink
>> and do justice and righteousness?
>>> Then it was well with him.
> He judged the cause of the poor and needy;
>> then it was well.
> Is not this to know me?
>> says the LORD. (Jeremiah 22.13–16)

Jeremiah is here condemning the king of Judah,

Jehoiakim (see 2 Kings 23.34–24.7), for his oppressive rule. Jehoiakim, he implies, aimed at self-aggrandisement rather than at establishing justice. Jeremiah contrasts him with his father Josiah (see 2 Kings 22.1–23.30). The oracle equates 'knowing God', not with a personal 'religious experience', but with practical deeds of 'justice and righteousness'. In the Old Testament this means both dispensing unbiased justice in cases of dispute, and providing help for the disenfranchised members of society such as widows and orphans. We could say that such a message is 'not political', if we meant to stress that it is cast in the form of an oracle from God, and is not a piece of human advice. But it would be better to say that it *is* political, since it reflects a belief that God is deeply concerned for the ordering of human society, and wishes earthly kingdoms to be ruled according to high moral standards.

Finally, here is an example from Micah:

Hear, you heads of Jacob
and rulers of the house of Israel!
Is it not for you to know justice?
  you who hate the good and love the evil,
who tear the skin from off my people,
  and their flesh from off their bones;
who eat the flesh of my people
  and flay their skin from off them,
and break their bones in pieces,
  and chop them up like meat in a kettle,
  like flesh in a cauldron.
Then they will cry to the LORD,
  but he will not answer them;
he will hide his face from them at that time,
  because they have made their deeds evil.

(Micah 3.1–4)

In this vivid metaphorical language the prophet attacks the rulers of Israel who exploit and abuse the poor who are in their power, treating them like so much meat to be eaten. Again, it is hard to see how one can avoid saying that this message is political.

The Old Testament prophets were influential figures in countries which were sovereign states – however small and insignificant – and they addressed the nation's rulers in the name of the one God both they and their hearers claimed to worship. The political message of the New Testament is very different, because the relation of Christian teachers to the state was so utterly different. The Christian church, during the period covered by the New Testament, was simply one among many religious sects in the Roman Empire, and Christianity was far less important socially and politically even than the Judaism within which it arose. It would be several centuries before Christianity established itself as the official religion of the Empire. So far as international politics is concerned, only the book of Revelation offers much in the way of comment, presenting the outcome of all wars and battles as resting in the hand of God, who will change the whole world order and make it subject to his Son:

> Then the seventh angel blew his trumpet, and there were loud voices in heaven, saying, 'The kingdom of the world has become the kingdom of our Lord and of his Christ, and he shall reign for ever and ever.' (Revelation 11.15)

For most of the New Testament period Christians were political outsiders in the places where they lived. The only question they had to answer was whether they should try to be good citizens of the pagan Empire, or should resist and oppose it. The books that bear the name of John (the Gospel, the three Epistles, and Revelation) see no common ground between Christians and unbelievers. Christians 'walk in the light', whereas 'the whole world is in the power of the evil one' (1 John 5.19). So Christians have no civic duties, and the pagan state has no claim on their allegiance, being an instrument of the devil. But in St Paul we find a much more positive attitude towards Roman administration:

> Let every person be subject to the governing authorities. For there is no authority except from God, and those that exist [AV: the powers that be] have been instituted by God. Therefore he who resists the authorities resists what God has appointed, and those who resist will incur judgement. For rulers are not a terror to good conduct, but to bad. Would you have no fear of him who is in authority? Then do what is good, and you will receive his approval, for he is God's servant for your good. But if you do wrong, be afraid, for he does not bear the sword in vain; he is the servant of God to execute his wrath on the wrongdoer. Therefore one must be subject, not only to avoid God's wrath but also for the sake of conscience. For the same reason you also pay taxes (Romans 13.1–6).

This text is often quoted by those who think Christians should never oppose the government under which they live. Certainly it does imply a high degree of subjection to 'the governing authorities'. But what would Paul have said if he found himself in a situation such as ours, in free Western democracies, where Christians do not have only to choose between obedience and rebellion but can actually influence the government and even form part of it? This is very hard to guess. Obeying a pagan magistrate is one thing, becoming a Christian magistrate is quite another. And on the whole Christians have found little to help them in the New Testament when seeking guidance for their political lives. The only recorded utterance of Jesus on the subject is the famous 'Render to Caesar the things that are Caesar's, and to God the things that are God's' (Matthew 22.21); and this is highly, perhaps intentionally, enigmatic. Some people quote it as a knock-down argument for complete submission to the government (because 'Caesar' has legitimate rights); but others take it to mean that though 'Caesar' has a limited claim on us, God has a total one. Everything, after all, 'belongs to God'. The chapter in Matthew's Gospel where the story appears, records a number of trick questions put to Jesus by his opponents, and in each case he replies by broadening the question and then, for the most part, giving a cryptic answer. The Gospels give us virtually no guidance on how the political life of a democracy should be conducted, still less one in which Christians are numerous and influential; we could hardly expect them to.

How, then, can the Bible contribute to modern political life, if the circumstances in which Old and New Testaments came into being were so different from each other, and both are so different from our own? Since there are so few rules in the Bible for the conduct of human political life, it has been commoner to look for places where the whole situation envisaged in the biblical text is close enough to our own for us to argue from it by analogy. For example, it may be accepted that the Bible tells us nothing about the duties and obligations of a welfare state, which no biblical author could have envisaged. At the same time, however, certain broad principles can be deduced from the cases of good government we find in the Bible, particularly in the Old Testament. In Jeremiah 22.13–16, the prophet condemns Jehoiakim and commends Josiah, showing that rulers should care for the poor and needy; and we may argue from this that callous indifference to the plight of less fortunate members of society is enough to disqualify any regime from the claim to be 'biblically' based. This does not, though, solve the *practical* question of how concern for the poor is best implemented. Some will say that a complete welfare state is needed; but others will retort that the poor are best served by allowing free market forces to operate, and relying on individual charity. Either way, it would be possible to condemn the kind of nation where the ruler pockets all the income of the country in order to build himself vast palaces, buy yachts, and become part of the international jet set; that mode of 'government' is certainly not 'biblical'. But this will not discriminate for us between socialist, social-democratic, or Tory policies, each of which would claim to be using the best available method of ensuring maximum prosperity for all.

In recent years a particularly powerful model has been identified in the Israelite experience of rescue from slavery in Egypt, wandering in the wilderness, and entry to the Promised Land. If we ask, 'Where is God in the political process?', then many influential thinkers would reply, 'He is where he was at the time of the exodus: on the side of the poor and oppressed against those who have enslaved them.' This is the recurring theme in the movement known as liberation theology. In Latin America especially, liberation theologians have applied the example of slavery in Egypt to their own experience of repressive regimes. They have identified the poor among whom they live and work with the oppressed Israelites, making bricks without pay for the king of Egypt. There are no *laws* in the Bible that say one should break out of slavery, or that authentic human existence is possible only when people refuse to be slaves and assert their human dignity. But the model of the Exodus has this as its most important implication.

The 'country' to which the poor of Latin America want to find their way is not literally a new land, as Canaan was for the Israelites; yet, at a metaphorical level, their destination is indeed another country. It is the country where they already live so changed and turned upside down as to be hardly recognisable. What they are seeking is a Latin America in which free and dignified human life is possible for all, because the exploitative structures of old and corrupt regimes have been entirely eliminated.

In his book *Liberation Theology*, Philip Berryman heads his section on this theme 'Exodus – Prototype of Liberation', and writes:

> Without a doubt, the exodus is the central event in the Hebrew Scriptures, the event that constitutes Israel as a people . . . When the pharaoh . . . pursues them, the waters return, drowning his troops. This act of deliverance is a basic paradigm of God's saving action.
>
> In a Latin American reading the focus is on God's concern to liberate the people, . . . This is a God who can hear the cry of the oppressed, who comes down, and who leads them to liberation. 'Exodus' is not simply an event but a pattern of deliverance that provides a key for interpreting the Scriptures and for interpreting present experience.[6]

We should notice that the use of biblical models can be a two-edged sword. The Stuart dynasty's dogma of the 'divine right of kings' did not rest on an appeal to a universal human belief in monarchy, nor on particular moral laws in the Bible; it rested on an appeal to the model of the Old Testament idea of the anointed king as sacrosanct. Little did David know, when he refused to kill his enemy Saul after he had him in his power, that he was establishing a precedent which would produce in England the disastrous years of the early seventeenth century, with a stubborn king claiming divine authority and a Parliament thinking it necessary to execute him. David had said (1 Samuel 24.6) 'The LORD forbid that I should do this thing to my lord, the LORD's anointed, to put forth my hand against him, seeing he is the Lord's anointed.' In Shakespeare's hands this alleged sacrosanctity of the monarch is shown to have been the downfall of Richard II, as it was to be of Charles I:

> Not all the water in the rough rude sea
>   Can wash the balm from an anointed king.
> The breath of worldly men cannot depose
> The deputy elected by the Lord.
>   (*Richard II*, Act 3, scene 2, lines 50–3.)

Probably almost no one now believes in the divine right of kings; yet the model has not ceased to be there in Scripture. Why, we may ask, is it illicit to use the Old Testament example of the anointed monarch, but allowable to use the illustration of the exodus? If the distinction is correct, it can only be because we know *from other sources* (reason, or tradition, or common sense) that God really is on the side of the poor (as Exodus says) but is not concerned with the persons of monarchs (as 1 Samuel implies). In this case it can fairly be noted that the books of Samuel also contain material which is hostile to the monarchy (e.g. 1 Samuel 12), whereas the Bible is never inconsistent about its 'bias to the poor'.

The ambiguities of this kind of argument do suggest that, even if we could treat biblical *laws* as absolutely and unequivocally binding, there is a question mark over treating biblical models in the same way. In applying biblical models to modern life, there is a great risk that we shall choose the ones that appeal to us, but then deceive ourselves into thinking that we decide as we do because the authority of Scripture is constraining us to do so. It might be more honest to admit that the biblical text, even if it is more than merely a convenient peg to hang a modern political theory on, is less than a full and perfect justification for liberation (or any other kind of political) theology. An appeal to biblical models can never have the character of a knock-down argument, but is at best illustrative or supportive of a conclusion reached on other grounds.

The case of the exodus is in fact a particularly good illustration of the dangers lurking in our path. Long before the arrival of liberation theology, exodus language was being used by American negroes in their own quest for liberation, and many spirituals bear witness to this:

> When Israel was in Egypt's land:
>> Let my people go;
> Oppressed so hard they could not stand:
>> Let my people go.
>>> Go down, Moses,
>> Way down in Egypt's land,
>>> Tell ole Pharaoh,
>>> Let my people go.

Such an equation between the enslaved Israelites and blacks in the USA was an everyday theme in the Civil Rights movement of the 1950s and 1960s. But, by a quirk of fate, the same exodus model was also traditionally used in South Africa by Afrikaners in their glorification of the Great Trek, with the blacks of southern Africa being cast in the role of the Canaanites who had to give way before the children of Israel. J.W. de Gruchy describes this use of the model as follows:

A defeated people need an interpretation of their history, a mythos, which can enable them to discover significance in what has happened to them. The continuity of the Afrikaner demanded such a world-view which would provide coherence to their shattered hopes. Such a mythos was not difficult to construct, especially for a people with such a strong belief in providence and an existential awareness of the plight of ancient Israel as it sought liberation from the Egyptian yoke. So it is not surprising that Afrikaner history, like that of other nations, took on a sacred character. . . . In their struggle against British imperialism, especially in the aftermath of the Anglo-Boer War, or the Second War of Independence, the Afrikaners drew immense strength from this interpretation of history. They detected a sacred thread running through all the events of their past, beginning with the Great Trek into the unknown (the exodus) and including the encounter with and victory over the black nations (Philistines), especially at the Battle of Blood River, where they entered into a sacred covenant with God, the entry into the promised land of the Transvaal and Orange Free State, and the encounter with the pursuing British.[7]

All this makes me chary of justifying political systems by appeals to biblical models. The danger of hearing from the Bible what we want to hear is simply too great. It is better, in my judgement, to say that the Bible offers relatively little guidance on questions of political conduct, and to use other sources, not least reason, to fill this gap. The Bible is not the be-all and end-all of the Christian faith. Attempts to make it so all too often twist it to ignoble ends, and mean that we do not hear it speaking with its own voice.

CHAPTER EIGHT

Is the Bible Sexist?

It has become the custom in both Catholic and Anglican churches for the person who has just read a passage from the Bible to conclude 'This is the Word of the Lord'. The congregation then replies, 'Thanks be to God'. This is a much more uplifting formula than the old, 'Here ends (endeth) the second lesson', which is true but trivial. Even so, the new system has its own drawbacks. Rather than identifying the whole Bible as God's 'word' in a rather general way – as in the formulas more common in Protestant churches, such as 'Hear this reading from God's Word' – it appears to imply that *this particular reading*, taken out of context, is the word that God is speaking at this moment to this particular congregation. In many cases there is no great problem about this. But to follow passages on certain themes with 'This is the Word of the Lord' causes either amusement or offence. Thus we get bits of pure historical narration, sayings in Proverbs, and commands to destroy Canaanites, not to mention those passages where Paul is actually *denying* that his advice is a word from the Lord (e.g. 1 Corinthians 7.12–16), all ending with this stock formula. And worst of all, in the minds of some, we find:

> As in all the churches of the saints, the women should keep silence in the churches. For they are not permitted to speak, but should be subordinate, even as the law says. If there is anything they desire to know, let

> them ask their husbands at home. For it is shameful
> for a woman to speak in church. (1 Corinthians
> 14.33–5)
>   This is the word of the Lord.

Some people are entirely happy with the formula after
such a passage, and we shall look at their point of view in
a moment. But other responses I have heard to such readings include 'This is supposed to be the word of the Lord',
'This is the word of St Paul', and 'Make up your own
minds whether this is the word of the Lord' – though so
far I have not yet heard 'This is *not* the word of the Lord'.

So-called 'sexist' passages in the Bible in fact only raise
in an acute form a general problem about the inspiration and authority of Scripture, and I should like to
discuss them with that wider issue always in mind. But
of course the issue is also an important one in itself. I
shall set out five ways of thinking about 'sexism' in
Scripture, each of which is important for a relatively
large group of people in the modern Church. We shall
see that in each case substantial issues going well
beyond the important question of the Bible's attitude to
the sexes quickly arise.

Are Women Subordinate?

'The Bible is what some people choose to call "sexist"
and quite right too.' The term 'sexism', to someone
who thinks like this, is already introducing (deliberate)
confusion, since it is obviously a derogatory term or
'boo-word'. The Bible does not support the strict
equality or equivalence of the sexes, because the Bible
correctly recognises that the sexes are not, in the nature
of things, equal or equivalent. The subordination of
woman to man is made explicit in Genesis 3, in the
story of the garden of Eden:

> To the woman he said, 'I will greatly multiply your pain in childbearing; in pain you shall bring forth children, yet your desire shall be for your husband, *and he shall rule over you.* (Genesis 3.16)

Although it is from the Bible that we can learn these facts about men and women, people who follow this first position will not usually say that equality of the sexes is wrong *because* the Bible condemns it. They are more likely to think that nature itself teaches the subordination of the female to the male, and if the Bible says so too, that just goes to prove how inspired the Bible is. St Paul uses the 'natural law' argument on such issues in 1 Corinthians 11.13, when dealing with the veiling of women in church:

> Judge for yourselves; is it proper for a woman to pray to God with her head uncovered? Does not nature itself teach you that for a man to wear long hair is degrading to him, but if a woman has long hair, it is her pride?

This high evaluation of the consonance between the Bible and what is 'natural' is especially common among two groups of people: traditional Catholics and fairly conservative evangelical Christians. For Catholics, there is a tendency for the 'natural law' argument to predominate, but its support from the inspired words of Scripture is welcomed and taken seriously. Evangelicals tend to call the Bible's teaching on the subordination of women a 'creation ordinance'. But by this is meant not only that such rulings occur in the context of the early chapters of Genesis, but also that they are built into the way the world is meant to be – God, of course, being the source of both the world and of Genesis. In both cases there is an appeal to human reason. The agreement between what can be deduced logically by observing how the world is and the evidence of Genesis or of St Paul provides two strands of an unbreakable cord. The Creator's intention, as deduced by observation of the world he has made, and as revealed in the Scriptures he has given us, is one and the same.

People who hold this view usually take care to say that they do not see women as inferior to men, but as different from them. The difference has theological, not merely practical, importance. They will sometimes point to the position in traditional Judaism, where the woman's role is quite different from the man's but is regarded (it is commonly claimed) as equally important. The Bible, they will stress, is far from regarding women as mere chattels, as some societies do: women have their own proper dignity in the Bible. But women remain the 'weaker vessel', and it is inappropriate for them to hold positions of leadership in the church or even, perhaps, in human society in general. For after all, 'Adam was formed first, then Eve; and Adam was not deceived, but the woman was deceived and became a transgressor. Yet the woman will be saved through bearing children, if she continues in faith and love and holiness, with modesty' (1 Timothy 2.13–15).

Some people, made of stern stuff, argue that 'the Bible must be followed even though it conflicts with human common sense'. For them, natural reason would lead in the direction of sexual equality, but the Bible condemns this, and that must be enough. One sees this type of position in some conservative forms of Judaism, where the different roles of the sexes in religious practice are justified on the basis that that is what the Torah reveals about God's will for his chosen people, never mind what human reason might want to say. Thus the existence of women rabbis, which in

Reform Judaism is a consequence of a commonsense 'why not?' argument, is seen by more traditional Jews as a blot on Jewish life. Jews should be governed by what the Torah says, not by what human beings think 'reasonable'.

Christian opposition to the ordination of women often has the same logic. It is acknowledged that reason has nothing to say against the practice, but the witness of Scripture contradicts mere human reason. Catholic (and Anglo-Catholic) opponents of ordaining women usually appeal to the fact that Jesus appointed only male apostles, and argue that his practice must be our example. Evangelicals more commonly argue that the New Testament explicitly opposes giving women authority over men. Since for them ordination is conceived very much as the conferring of authority to order the church's affairs, this makes women's ordination inconceivable. On similar grounds they argue that a husband should have authority over his wife: not exercising this authority coercively or without love, but remaining in the last resort the partner who makes large decisions about job, home, and family:

> Wives, be subject to your husbands, as to the Lord. For the husband is the head of the wife as Christ is the head of the church, his body, and is himself its Saviour. . . . Husbands, love your wives, as Christ loved the church. . . . Let each one of you love his wife as himself, and let the wife see that she respects her husband. (Ephesians 5.22–33)

This is not a picture of harsh or unyielding authority, but rather of a bond of love. But in the last resort if there is a disagreement, it is the husband who gives a ruling.

The opposite position to this is to say: 'The Bible *is*

sexist; but that does not mean we have to be.' Christians who wish to argue in this way quickly find that the version of Christianity which they hold to has a loose, rather than a tight, connection with the biblical text. They have to maintain that the Christian faith, though related in some rather subtle way to Scripture, is far from being tightly constrained by it. Such is the position normally referred to as 'liberal', and it is close to the underlying tone of the present book, as some readers will by now have realised. From this point of view we might not want to say that the Bible is 'sexist' – a highly emotive word, which has the effect of rubbishing anything it is applied to. But we would freely concede that in the case of relations between the sexes the Bible is very far from the general consensus in western 'liberalism'. So what? is the next question. Modern Christians have the right and, indeed, the obligation to formulate matters of Christian faith and ethics in the light not only of 'tradition' (which includes the Bible) but also in the light of the best insights of the modern world. How far modern culture should be allowed to modify the tradition, and how far the tradition should be used to challenge modern culture, is a deeply interesting and important question. But there is no universal, blanket answer to it which we can apply mechanically. The rights of women are one very clear example (it is said) where modern thinking has the capacity to modify what has come down to us from the Christian past, including what is in the Bible. It is a caricature of this to say that, for a 'liberal' Christian or Jew, the Bible is quite sexist but that does not matter a bit. But there is certainly a willingness to allow that progress can be made in moral debate, and that this is an issue on which progress has indeed been made. Our view of the authority of Scripture must then be adjusted, so as to show that the change in Christian or Jewish thinking which has in fact happened is not incompatible with a continuing reverence for the Bible. This is a difficult but not necessarily an impossible task.

On the other hand, there are some who say 'the Bible is sexist, and Christians are committed to the Bible; so I cannot be a Christian.' People who think this way reject the sophisticated arguments of liberals as merely a way of trying to have one's cake and eat it too. They see this is an intellectually dishonest way of updating the Christian faith by making it up to suit ourselves. As T.S. Eliot memorably put it, 'Christianity is always adapting itself into something which can be believed': hardly an intellectually honest procedure! Far better, they would say, to face the fact that the Bible is incorrigibly hostile to women, and stop pretending that a feminist can also be a Christian. Like the conservative approaches with which we began, this has the great virtue of simplicity; you know where you are with it. I do not think I should be writing this book if I believed that this was the only honest position, but its challenge to more 'woolly' Christians is clear, and it deserves more of a hearing than Christians commonly give it.

So far we have looked at positions which assume the Bible is indeed 'sexist', though some would object to that way of putting it. But there are many biblical scholars who would seriously question whether the Bible really does accord such a lowly place to women as we have been assuming. When seen against its cultural background, in a society where the dominance of men was entirely taken for granted, the Bible turns out to be considerably less sexist than one might expect. Old Testament law, for instance, may not make men and women equal before the courts, but it does entrench a number of rights which women certainly did not have elsewhere in the ancient Middle East. This is especially true of some significant changes introduced in the book of Deuteronomy (perhaps from the seventh century BC) as against its primary underlying source, the (possibly tenth-century) 'Book of the Covenant' (Exodus 21–3). Thus the Book of the Covenant provides that certain kinds of slave, probably those who had been enslaved because they could not pay their debts, should be released in the seventh year after being enslaved. But this applies only to men; as to women, they 'shall not go out as the male slaves do' – though even here there are provisions to prevent the slave-owner from treating them oppressively (see Exodus 21.1–11). Deuteronomy, however, says that male and female slaves are to be treated equally in respect of release (Deuteronomy 15.12–18). What is more, slaves of either sex are not to be released into penury; for that might give them little real option but to stay on in service. They are to be liberally provisioned to tide them over after their release; and this applies as much to women as to men (Deuteronomy 15.17b).

Deuteronomy also introduces a subtle but significant change into the Ten Commandments. In Exodus we read 'You shall not covet your neighbour's house; you shall not covet your neighbour's wife, or his manservant, or his maidservant, or his ox, or his ass, or anything that is your neighbour's' (20.17) – the wife is apparently just another chattel. But Deuteronomy says 'Neither shall you covet your neighbour's wife; and you shall not desire your neighbour's house, his field, or his manservant, or his maidservant, his ox, or his ass, or anything that is your neighbour's' (5.12). Here the wife appears first, and is differentiated from the other things, which are possessions in a sense that she is not.

In the New Testament, we should note, the only

place where Jesus rules on the rights of women is also in connection with marriage. He tightens up the Mosaic law on divorce and argues that man and woman should be 'one flesh', inseparable for life. This had the effect of making his followers abandon Jewish marriage customs, according to which a man had an absolute right to divorce his wife (provided only that he might not leave her destitute), and to substitute a much more rigorous practice. Jesus' teaching in theory gives married women more security; though in modern conditions we are bound to see its potential for locking them irrevocably into a loveless marriage. Jesus' own conduct clearly bespeaks a great liking and respect for women, many of whom were prominent among his followers (see Mark 15.40–1; Luke 7.36–8.3, 23.55–6; John 11). It is only with St Paul that we begin to meet restrictions on women's place in the church. This tendency is taken further in the Pastoral Epistles (1 and 2 Timothy and Titus), which most scholars regard as an imitation of Paul by one of his followers rather than as the work of the apostle himself. Here we may look for special explanations of what is, in any case, not a consistent trend. For example, there was the danger of giving scandal if churches were known to be places where women had a freedom of action inconsistent with the restrictions on them in Greek society at large; the risk, especially in the seamier parts of a city such as Corinth, that complete mixing of the sexes in worship might precipitate a return to the kind of orgiastic rites which the Corinthian Christians had only recently cast off; even, perhaps, excessively 'charismatic' tendencies among particular women in the Corinthian church, which could be dealt with only by adopting what looks like a harsh, blanket policy of keeping women silent. All the same, Paul's arguments from 'what nature itself teaches' do not suggest a man at ease with women exercising any kind of authority. The Pastoral Epistles, especially in the reference to Adam and Eve cited above, are more obviously misogynistic: it is scandalously untrue that 'Adam was not deceived' but only Eve. Interestingly, the Old Testament contains very little overt misogyny of this sort – Eve in any case is not mentioned after Genesis 3. However much Old Testament texts require the subordination of women, hatred of them very rarely surfaces. Only in some of the 'wisdom' books do we find advice to young men to avoid wicked women, and even then the reference is usually to prostitution and adultery, not to relations with women as such. It is not until late in the Old Testament period that a disagreeable misogyny emerges clearly. 'Do not sit in the midst of women; for from garments comes the moth, and from a woman comes woman's wickedness. Better is the wickedness of a man than a woman who does good, and it is a woman who brings shame and disgrace' (Ecclesiasticus 42.12–14). The New Testament, however, is not so unequivocally sexist as people often think; and against the culture of its time, it is surprisingly 'enlightened', at least in places.

All the positions summarised so far assume that the Bible's attitude towards women is different, and less 'liberal', than in a modern culture which has lived for many years with feminism of various kinds. However, there are people who would argue that this is far from being the case. On the contrary, the few passages we have quoted as restricting the actions of women are no more than occasional blots on a book which is mostly, and in an ancient context quite remarkably, open to the needs and rights of women.

Despite the rather grudging character of many of the laws, it is clear from the Old Testament that in many periods women occupied positions of considerable power and influence. The queen and the queen mother were major personages at the court of Israelite and Judaean kings. What is more, many of the older, more legendary accounts of the times of the patriarchs (in Genesis) present a picture of extremely strong-minded and independent women. One recent writer observes with some justice that in one strand in the Pentateuch there are no heroes, only heroines;[8] while from a later period, the little 'tales' in the Old Testament and Apocrypha often have women as their central characters: Esther, Judith, Ruth. There is also a lengthy description of the 'virtuous woman' in Proverbs 31 which assumes that she will engage in business and keep her family by independent enterprise in which her husband seems to play no part.

> She considers a field and buys it;
>   with the fruit of her hands she plants a vineyard,
> She girds her loins with strength
>   and makes her arms strong.

> She opens her hand to the poor,
>   and reaches out her hands to the needy.

> Strength and dignity are her clothing,
>   and she laughs at the time to come.
> She opens her mouth with wisdom,
>   and the teaching of kindness is on her tongue.

Many of the best-drawn characters in the historical books are women, and they are extremely capable, far-sighted and assertive. There is Abigail, the wise wife of a stupid husband (1 Samuel 25); Deborah, who leads the people into battle (Judges 4); and Tamar, who gets the better of the patriarch Judah and is praised by him for it in the words 'She is more righteous than I' (Genesis 38).

But it is in the New Testament that we see the really profound change in the evaluation of women which the Christian movement produced (though it lost it again even before the New Testament library was complete, as we can see from the Pastoral Epistles). St Paul, for all his caution in the Corinthian letters, shows elsewhere that he had come to accept a very radical position about the place of women:

> As many of you as were baptised into Christ have put on Christ. There is neither Jew nor Greek, there is neither slave nor free, there is neither male nor female; for you are all one in Christ Jesus. (Galatians 3.27–8)

Just as the church contained both Jews and Gentiles, yet abolished the distinctions between them, so, Paul is arguing, the difference between men and women has no relevance in the church's life. This does not, admittedly, automatically mean that their roles are identical, but it does make it hard to see how in practice he can have maintained the strict differentiation insisted on in 1 Corinthians. The church is a society which levels all distinctions. This is a precious Pauline insight whose radical nature must not be ignored.

Consistently with this, Paul evidently had a lot of female co-workers in establishing the churches he founded. Romans 16 names Phoebe, Prisca, Mary, Junia, Tryphaena and Tryphosa, and Julia. Philippians 4.1—2 adds Euodia and Syntyche, and says that 'they have laboured side by side with me in the gospel together with Clement and the rest of my fellow workers, whose names are in the book of life.' Colossians 4.15 speaks of Nympha 'and the church in her house'. One begins to get the impression that, in a broadly 'sexist' culture, the Christian community was experimenting with fresh patterns and structures in which women played a significant role, on a basis of equality with male leaders. Very soon traditional models reasserted themselves, and women returned to playing a subordinate role. But at the beginning of the Christian movement the freedom of the gospel asserted itself in a quite new style of relationship between the sexes, with women playing a leading role as much as men.

This seems broadly in keeping with the ministry of Jesus himself. One often hears it said that 'all the apostles were men', and this is true as far as it goes. A peripatetic band of people including women on an equal footing is very hard to imagine in first-century Palestine, where the women would have been assumed to be prostitutes. Nevertheless the Gospels record a quite extraordinary involvement of women in the course of Jesus' ministry – some of whom did in fact follow Jesus from Galilee to Jerusalem, and some of them probably *were* prostitutes, discovering for the first time a man who enjoyed their company and showed them the forgiving love of God, instead of using their services. Women, according to the Gospels, were the earliest witnesses to the resurrection – though at first, rather predictably, no-one believed them. Early Christianity seems to have been unusually 'non-sexist' in style. And that, surely, should influence the modern Christian more strongly than occasional texts from later New Testament Epistles.

Is God Male?

So far we have concentrated on the position of women in the Bible. I have tried to set out some possible lines of interpretation, and am sure that my own preferences have become clear. I propose to leave this subject there, and encourage readers to look at the texts themselves and draw their own conclusions. But so far I have skirted round the other question which feminist readers of the Bible have brought to the forefront of attention. This question is: Is *God* male?

To put it briefly, the same five positions may be found on this question as on the Bible's attitude to women.

No intelligent person, I suppose, thinks that God is *literally* male – that he has a body with male sexual organs. But many people think that the Bible's depiction of him as male, and its use of male pronouns to refer to him, captures something about God more truly than feminine language would. God as we know him by reason and reflection has qualities which in human beings are associated with power, control, and taking initiatives, and this (it may be said) means that to speak of him other than in male terms would be seriously misleading. People who think like this are generally fairly clear in their minds about which qualities in human beings are 'masculine' and 'feminine', and if the distinction is applied to God, he will emerge as (metaphorically speaking) like a man rather than like a woman.

Others believe that we cannot know anything of God unless he reveals himself to us; he cannot be known through human reason. Hence we cannot say, on the basis of human reflection alone, whether God is 'male' or 'female'; we must wait to be told by God him/herself. But we have been told. The Bible reveals clearly that God prefers us to think of him as male, and we are not at liberty to challenge this revelation on any grounds whatever.

On the other hand, there are those who believe that the emphasis in Scripture on the maleness of God is a reason either for rejecting the Bible altogether, as a book which enshrines all the worst effects of patriarchy – giving comfort to those who oppress woman, and encouraging men in machismo; or else that in this respect the Bible has only relative authority for Christians. Modern insights, it may be said, have revealed that the nature of God is either more 'female' or more 'neutral' than the Bible allows; but we can go on using the Bible, because we can discount and make allowances for its 'male' slant. We can see that this is an accident of history. The Bible's 'message' is for all time, but features belonging to the specific cultural context(s) in which it was written are not. This is like the 'liberal' position described earlier: 'Yes, the God of the Bible is (generally) presented as male, but don't let that worry you: not everything in Scripture has eternal validity.'

It is possible to see ways in which the God of the Bible is less 'male' than adherents of all these various positions suppose. Ancient Israelites undoubtedly believed that if they were ever to see God, they would see a male figure. (Of course they did not expect to do so, the vision of God being a very rare gift.) Ezekiel's vision of God (Ezekiel 1–2 and 8) is unequivocal here. Ezekiel says, in a very roundabout way, that he saw 'a form that had the appearance of a man' (Ezekiel 8.2). If one could see God, one would see something male in appearance, not female. In that sense Yahweh, as God is called in the Old Testament, is a 'male' God. But the qualities possessed by this divine being are not described, in the Old Testament, in exclusively male terms. God cares for Israel like a mother (Isaiah 49.14–15); the love with which he 'carries' his people into the Promised Land speaks of gentle leading, not 'male' coercion (Isaiah 63.7–14); and in much of the Bible, though 'masculine' verbs and pronouns (in the grammatical sense) are applied to God, there is no insistence on them as essential.

They are the form you use when you are not positively insisting that someone is female – just as in English (till a few years ago) masculine pronouns were not felt to exclude women unless this was clearly being insisted on.

Feminists have argued forcefully that such linguistic customs, however 'innocent', give a subliminal 'slant' to a language: they imply that the male is 'normal', the female a deviation from it. That there is something in this I do not for a moment doubt. But in Hebrew, where (as in French) there are only two grammatical genders, one has to choose one or the other. English has no *grammatical* gender at all, only a few forms – such as personal pronouns – that indicate the *sex* of the person being referred to ('he', 'she', etc.). Ordinary nouns have no gender at all, and this makes it hard for a native English speaker to grasp that the sex of a person or animal is not being insisted on by the gender of the word used, in languages which do have grammatical gender. Thus, to take a famous case, we think it odd that the French for a (male) sentry is *une sentinelle*, and that the German for a girl (*Mädchen*) is neuter. But speakers of these languages do not find it particularly odd at all, since they do not expect any but the loosest correlation between gender and sex. Hebrew culture was far from unusual in regarding the masculine gender as inclusive in a way that the feminine was not. We may not like it, but we cannot do anything about it. And it certainly ought not to blind us to the considerable use made of 'feminine' imagery in the Bible's picture of God. See, for example, Isaiah 49.15: 'Can a woman forget her sucking child, that she should have no compassion on the son of her womb? Even these may forget; yet I will not forget you'.

So far as the divine realm is concerned, Hebrew culture increasingly set its face against the worship of any God but Yahweh. The rejection of feminine epithets for

God may well be linked to this monotheistic tendency. If there is only one divine being, then, in the thought-world of the ancient Middle East, that being will be thought of as either male or female. Hebrew culture rejected the possibility that the sole divine being might be a goddess. This rejection of goddesses is tightly connected with a rejection of 'fertility' religion, with its orgiastic practices. Some feminists believe strongly that this was itself a mistake: fertility religion has much to commend it, they think. But anyone who does not think this must recognise that in the ancient context, the only means of expressing opposition to such religion produced, as a necessary even if unintended consequence, a picture of God as male. It also, incidentally, required people to believe that this God had no consort – a very strange idea in the ancient Near East. A male god but with no partner is about as close as one could come, in that culture, to a god from whose life sexuality is altogether excluded, and is a significant step along the road to a full monotheism, in which the God who is worshipped is 'without body, parts, or passions'; as the Church of England's Thirty-Nine Articles of Religion puts it.

> The essential dissonance is not between the Old Testament and femininity but between the Old Testament and nature religion. The conflict is between Old Testament theology, which acknowledges God's radical transcendence of the world which he has made, on the one hand, and, on the other hand, fertility-cult notions which confuse the Creator with the creature by implying that the deity partakes in human sexuality. Thus, both the feminists who venerate a female deity and those who react against this by stressing the maleness of God are revitalising the unhealthy emphases of the fertility cultures which the

> Old Testament roundly condemns. They are depart-
> ing from faith in a transcendent Creator and Re-
> deemer and re-mythologizing – even re-magicalizing
> – religion.[9]

Speaking personally, I believe that modern Christians
need some way of expressing their continuity with the
religion of Israel in its rejection of polytheism, without
adopting the heavily 'male' language about God which,
at that time, was a necessary corollary. To insist that
God was 'male' in the sixth century BC was the only
way to avoid paganism. To insist that he is so today is to
take a far more stridently aggressive line against much
in contemporary religious thought. Paradoxically, in ancient times Yahweh, a 'male' god, presided over almost
the only ancient religion which included men and
women on anything like equal terms: Judaism and its
offshoot, Christianity. It is strange to find this liberating
insight now being used to exclude women from positions of authority in the Christian church which claims
to continue the traditions of the Bible.

Conclusion

Is the Bible sexist? We have seen that this question
involves both matters of substance and matters of definition. It also leads us very quickly into wider questions
of the nature and authority of the Bible, and the fascinating problem, for a Christian reader, of which
elements in the Bible are of permanent value as they
stand, which need to be reinterpreted, and which (if
any) need to be simply abandoned. It is not hard to see
that there are many other issues which would raise similar problems, but the question of 'sexism' is at the
moment the place where the shoe pinches most in the
Western churches.

CHAPTER NINE

Reading the Bible

'Begin at the beginning,' the King said, very gravely, 'and go on till you come to the end; then stop.' The King of Hearts' advice to the White Rabbit in *Alice in Wonderland* is adopted by many people who decide to read the Bible seriously and systematically. They begin with Genesis 1, and look forward to the day when they will reach Revelation 22.

Unfortunately most people who attempt this task fall by the wayside. Exciting tasks, of course, often begin to pall as we get into them, and turn into boring routine. But with the Bible there is a particular reason why so many people give up. Genesis, and the first twenty-four chapters of Exodus, are interesting enough by any standards. They are full of great sonorous passages like the creation stories in Genesis 1 and 2, and well-told tales such as the story of Joseph (Genesis 37–50), not to mention traditional favourites such as Moses in the bullrushes (Exodus 2.1–10). But after that the going gets distinctly tougher. At Exodus 25 we enter the great central block of legislation in the Pentateuch, which concentrates almost exclusively on the exact detail of complex religious rituals. You will find this interesting if you like discovering how great institutions run – if you are a lawyer concerned with constitutional law, an historian of national institutions, or a particular kind of traditional Catholic who likes reading about the ritual side of religion. There is no doubt in my mind that Exodus 25 to Numbers 15 is profoundly interesting.

But for most people it is an acquired taste; and most would-be Bible readers falter, and abandon the project somewhere in the middle of Leviticus. Those who persevere are rewarded by some splendid passages in Deuteronomy, and then the whole long tale of Israel's entry into the Promised Land. But for most people by then it is too late.

Aids to Bible Reading

There are a lot of aids to Bible reading that approach the text in a different way, and make it rather more likely that people will stay the course. First and foremost, both the Catholic and the Anglican Churches provide a daily lectionary. In the case of the Catholic Church, in fact, there are two: one which is included in the church's daily Office, and another, perhaps more accessible to most people, in the daily Missal, where every day of the year has its own special readings. In Anglicanism the lectionary for Morning and Evening Prayer covers most of the Bible in one year: the most recent edition (in England) is in the *Alternative Service Book 1980*. One advantage of church lectionaries is that, although each book of the Bible is read through consecutively (with some omissions), there is always both an Old and a New Testament reading. One does not have to wait till the end of Malachi before being allowed to begin the New Testament. There are certain traditions in the Western church, taken over in these lectionaries, that particular books should be read at particular times of the year. For example, Isaiah is traditionally read in Advent as part of the run-up to Christmas; Genesis and Exodus are read before Easter; the Acts of the Apostles is read in Eastertide. Using a lectionary means that you do not 'begin at the beginning', but it greatly increases the likelihood that you will 'go on to the end'.

A second resource for anyone intending to read the whole Bible are various books of selections from the Bible, which abbreviate and remove all the repetitions and untidiness of the original text. It is customary for a certain kind of Christian to sneer at these as 'mutilated' or 'easy' Bibles, but I cannot for the life of me see what is wrong with them. One of the best is the *Reader's Digest Bible Illustrated*, a 'condensed' edition of the Revised Standard Version, produced in the attractive format we have come to expect from Reader's Digest atlases and reference books. Among other 'abridged' Bibles I have noticed *The One Year Bible* and *The Bible in One Year*.[10] These two are, in effect, lectionaries, but every passage of the Bible is included in a single-year cycle, which many will find a rather rich diet. They have the oddity (among lectionaries) of paying no heed to religious festivals such as Christmas Day. In this category of abridged Bibles children's editions should not be ignored, though the drawback there is that they are commonly paraphrases rather than the 'real' Bible set out in a more helpful way. Among them A.T. Dale's *Winding Quest* and *New Life* (London 1972) probably remain the best on the market.

'Begin at the beginning' could be given a different interpretation: not 'begin with Genesis', but 'begin with the earliest texts to be written'. As I hope this book has made clear, dating portions of the Bible is a hazardous and uncertain task: no one can say *for sure* which is the oldest part of the Bible. But it is certainly not Genesis 1. By deliberately trying to read the biblical text in chronological order we can take seriously the historical dimension I have made much of in previous chapters. There is widespread agreement among biblical specialists that the very oldest parts of the Old Testament are a few poems: the victory hymn in

Judges 5, praising God for the victory over Sisera (probably from the twelfth century BC); the lament of David on the death of Saul and Jonathan at the battle of Gilboa in 2 Samuel 1.19–27 (eleventh century); and probably the 'last words' of David in 2 Samuel 23.1–7 (early tenth century). There used to be a consensus (proving more rickety in the last few years) that the story of Solomon's succession to the throne of David, 2 Samuel 9–20 and 1 Kings 1–2 – generally known as the 'Court History' or the 'Succession Narrative' – is more or less contemporary with the events it chronicles, and thus dates from no later than about 900 BC. The same has been argued for the oldest strand in the Pentateuch, which contains most of the well-told stories that keep the reader going through Genesis and the first half of Exodus, and which returns to prominence after Numbers 16 to refresh the reader who has actually succeeded in reading Leviticus. One of the most interesting Bible-publishing ventures of the last decade or so was Joseph Rhymer's *The Bible in Order*, which rearranged the text of the *Jerusalem Bible* into chronological order. No two scholars agree on exactly what order should be followed, but the general consensus is large enough to have made this a perfectly sensible attempt, and one which gave many readers a wholly new perspective on biblical literature. In the case of the New Testament it was intriguing to find the Epistle of James put first, on the grounds that this is essentially a pre-Christian Jewish work only slightly edited to fit it for a Christian Bible. But even if one discounts this possibility, the next work in the New Testament turned out to be 1 Thessalonians, and on that virtually all scholars would agree. *All St Paul's epistles are older than any of the Gospels.* A huge adjustment of perspective is needed to accommodate this (in the scholarly world) quite uncontroversial truth: to see it presented by the actual format of a Bible is a most salutary shock.

Not everyone will wish to read the Bible chronologically, even if they are convinced that the scholars can be trusted. Some may prefer to work through it thematically, or by types of literature. For the benefit of the castaway with whom this book began, who cannot buy any of these aids to Bible-reading, Appendix 3 and Appendix 4 presents two schemes for getting through substantial parts of the Bible, one chronological, the other by genre. Obviously they have no kind of authority, and can be used or left as the reader likes.

Which Translation?

Finding the right Bible translation for one's own needs is not easy. There are now two traditions of biblical translation in English. The first goes back to (indeed beyond) the *Authorised* (or *King James*) *Version*. The Authorised Version was not a new translation, but a revision of existing English versions, as the translators made explicit in their Preface:

> Truly, good Christian Reader, we never thought from the beginning that we should need to make a new translation, nor yet to make of a bad one a good one; . . . but to make a good one better, or out of many good ones one principal good one, not justly to be excepted against; that hath been our endeavour, that our mark.

They compared existing English translations with the original Hebrew and Greek (so far as proper critical editions of these were accessible to them). The result was an extraordinarily good translation, which continues to be enjoyed today. What they produced has a

147

good claim to be 'the Bible' of the English-speaking world – much as Luther's Bible is for German Protestants.

In 1882 the churches in England commissioned a revision of the AV in the light of recent scholarship, and the result was the Revised Version, a translation now almost forgotten, though we still used it for Theology examinations in Oxford until the early 1980s. One of its merits was that it aimed to be close enough, word-by-word, to the original languages to act as a kind of 'crib'. If you knew Hebrew or Greek you could practically reconstruct the underlying text from this very literal translation. At the same time, of course, it incorporated knowledge about the text which had not been known to King James' translators, the fruits of several centuries of good biblical scholarship.

This tradition continues in the Revised Standard Version, a revision of the American Standard Version of 1901, which was the American equivalent of the RV. The RSV (1952), now one of the most widely-used of all Bibles, retains the characteristic style and dignity of the AV, while going much further than any previous version in trying to give an intelligible meaning even to very obscure parts of the text. It has proved especially durable for reading in public. In 1990 there appeared a further revision, the New Revised Standard Version, which departs rather more from the AV tradition, particularly in such matters as the use of 'inclusive' language and of 'you' instead of 'thou' in addressing God.

The second tradition dates only from this century. It involves an attempt to translate the Bible 'from scratch', forging a new style instead of retaining the 'biblical English' of the AV-RSV tradition. The two principal monuments to this trend are the Catholic Jerusalem Bible (London, 1966), now revised as the New

Jerusalem Bible (NJB; 1985), and the New English Bible, the result of collaboration between scholars representing all the main non-Catholic churches. The JB was originally translated from the French *Bible de Jérusalem*, produced by scholars at the French Dominican École Biblique in Jerusalem, though the English translators referred constantly to the Hebrew and Greek originals. The NEB has now been succeeded by the Revised English Bible (1990), and to this Catholic scholars have contributed alongside their Protestant colleagues, so that it can claim to be the first ever fully ecumenical Bible in English. The JB-NJB/NEB-REB style has attracted much hostile criticism from those wedded to the beauty of the AV, but it is by now becoming more familiar in churches of all kinds. Indeed, there are now Christians who are quite unfamiliar with the AV except, perhaps, in snatches read on highly traditional occasions.

Alongside these two main traditions we may note also a tendency in very recent times for evangelical scholars to produce their own versions of the Bible, purged of what they see as tendentious translation by 'critical' specialists. The chief example is the New International Version (NIV), used by millions of Christians worldwide. Its style is generally in tune with the RSV, but it tends (seen from my personal perpective) to hide problems from the reader by choosing translations that smooth over difficulties (especially inconsistencies) in the text. In this it rather resembles some traditional Catholic translations, which used to be copiously provided with footnotes to warn the reader off interpretations incompatible with Catholic dogma. For example, references to Jesus' brothers and sisters in the Gospels were traditionally glossed as references to his 'cousins', to safeguard the church's teaching about the perpetual virginity of the Blessed Virgin. This occurs even in an edition of the RSV, the so-called Common Bible, which was meant for use by both Catholics and Protestants. In joining the panel that produced the REB and promoting its use by Catholics, the Catholic hierarchy has now effectively abandoned this tradition, for the REB has no notes at all except (like all other modern Bibles) where the text is obscure or uncertain in meaning. The NIV, on the other hand, puts its glosses into the text as though they were the only possible correct translations.

The JB and the NEB were not absolute pioneers. Earlier this century *A New Translation of the Bible* enjoyed some popularity. The New Testament was published in 1913, the Old in 1924, and a complete edition (but omitting the Apocrypha) followed in 1935. The translator was James Moffatt (1870–1944), a minister of the Free Church of Scotland who also taught for a time at Mansfield College, Oxford. Its style was somewhat florid and paraphrastic, and some of its decisions about appropriate equivalents now look dated: for example, the divine name 'Yahweh', traditionally rendered 'the LORD', appears throughout the Old Testament as 'the Eternal', often with a very lumbering effect. But its practical effectiveness in some places can be seen from the translation of 1 Corinthians 13:

> Love is very patient, very kind. Love knows no jealousy; love makes no parade, gives itself no airs, is never rude, never selfish, never irritated, never resentful; love is never glad when others go wrong, love is gladdened by goodness, always slow to expose, always eager to believe the best, always hopeful, always patient.

When I was confirmed I was given a small manual of prayers in which this passage from Moffatt was suggested as providing a useful means for examining one's conscience before receiving Holy Communion. It still seems to me much better than almost all the traditional checklists of sins. For it provides, not a list of prohibitions, but a description of the Christian character that we ought to be aiming at. It has to be admitted, though, that it is not all that close to what St Paul wrote.

J.B. Phillips also produced memorable translations of the whole New Testament, and towards the end of his life also of some parts of the Old. In his work too we see a desire to break free of the AV tradition, and forge a distinctively modern style for the Bible in English. One problem with deliberately 'modern' English is that it dates quickly, and some of Phillips's renderings now sound hopelessly time-bound (and class-bound) – as when the traditional 'Friend, go up higher' (Luke 14.10) becomes 'My dear fellow, we have a much better seat than that for you.' Nevertheless, especially in his translations of St Paul's epistles (called illuminatingly *Letters to Young Churches*) Phillips caught something of the freshness of the early Christian movement in a way rarely encountered in any other translation.

Controversy about these matters will continue. The best advice I can give someone beginning to read the Bible for the first time is: use the RSV or NRSV if traditional style matters to you; if not, use the NJB or REB. To my mind the REB has the edge over all other 'modern-language' translations, but the NJB has the advantage of helpful (and now untendentious) footnotes, introductions to the different books, and indexes. Once you are thoroughly familiar with the contents of the Bible, it may be time to turn back to an older version, since you will then be able to crosscheck where it lapses (as the AV quite often does) into total obscurity. It would be a pity if a whole generation of people were never made aware of the stylistic marvels in the AV, but this is not best secured by refusing them the help in Bible reading that only more modern versions can provide.

Systematic Study

Why should anyone want to embark on a systematic course of Bible reading anyway? The assumption throughout this book has been simply that the Bible is endlessly fascinating, and that mere curiosity about one of the monuments of world literature will be enough to make one want to read it. In this chapter I have been admitting that to the uninitiated (and in places even to the initiated) it has its tedious passages, so that one needs a bit of help if one is not to give up too soon. But of course I realise that many people want to read the Bible for religious reasons, because it is the vital foundation document of the Christian faith. They expect to find in it not merely some interesting writings, but the word of life. Since I am myself a Christian, I share this expectation; though it will have become evident that I do not think one need always approach Scripture in such a reverent frame of mind as to ignore or blank out its many imperfections and inconsistencies. It is not a book written by the hand of God, which dropped from heaven. It is a compendium of human *responses* to God's 'input' into the human situation.

Nevertheless, some readers may feel that I have not said enough about the use of the Bible for what might be called 'spiritual reading'. For those who wish to use short passages as a basis for prayer and meditation, there are many excellent books available. The Bible Reading Fellowship produces notes which carry one through substantial parts of the Bible by a day-by-day reading with short and helpful commentaries. These help to ensure that one does not get bogged down for too long in one particular section of the Bible, but has a mixed diet of Old and New Testaments, of narrative, poetry, Gospels, and epistles. The Scripture Union produces similar notes from a more clearly evangelical perspective. There are also many books which take the reader through passages of Scripture in an ordered way. Among them I especially like Delia Smith's two books *A Feast for Lent* and *A Feast for Advent*, written from the perspective of a very ecumenically-minded Catholic and published by the Bible Reading Fellowship.

Readers who have already acquired reasonable familiarity with what is in the Bible might want to begin serious study of it, and for this a reliable guide is needed. To my mind the best way in to more advanced study is provided by two books published by Lion, John Drane's *Introducing the Old Testament* and *Introducing the New Testament* (now available combined as *An Introduction to the Bible*, 1990). Anyone who reads these books and takes the time to look up and read every passage Drane comments on in detail, will have a thorough working knowledge both of the Bible, in its historical and cultural setting, and of modern theories about it. Drane's approach is moderately 'conservative', but by no means uncritical; and it seems to me that a basically quite conservative approach provides the best way to start studying the Bible, even if in time one finds oneself coming to somewhat more 'radical' conclusions about questions of date, authorship, and inspiration.

A further possibility, where the Old Testament is concerned, is to use three of the volumes of the Clarendon Bible series from Oxford University Press: E.W. Heaton's *The Hebrew Kingdoms* (1968), P.R. Ackroyd's *Israel Under Babylon and Persia* (1970), and D.S. Russell's *The Jews from Alexander to Herod* (1967). These

153

books cover between them the whole sweep of the history of Israel from the division of the kingdom on the death of Solomon (in the tenth century BC) down to the New Testament period. Again, specific passages belonging to each period are discussed in detail, and by looking each one up, and following it with the 'potted' commentary provided, readers can acquire a good basic knowledge of the Old Testament. There is nothing quite so convenient for the New Testament apart from Drane's book, but many people are helped by A.E. Harvey's short book *Something Overheard* (BRF 1977), which examines the setting and the religious and social issues that called forth the New Testament writings. Also excellent is his much longer *Companion to the New English Bible New Testament*, (Oxford and Cambridge 1970). As a background to all these works some people find the *Illustrated Bible* (available in AV, RSV, and NEB) useful. The illustrations, by Horace Knowles, are not merely decorative (sometimes they are not decorative at all) but include small sketch maps in the text wherever a journey or a location is being described, and also illustrate some unfamiliar objects such as cherubim, scrolls, or the Temple.

Everything I have written so far in this chapter implies that historical study of the Bible should be the norm: placing books in their correct historical setting, noting changes over time in biblical thought, trying to discover what the biblical authors *meant*. Because so many books in the Bible are composite, these are difficult tasks. But I have assumed that they are worthwhile ones. Even in speaking about 'spiritual' reading I have been taking it for granted (as is also the case, for example, in the Bible Reading Fellowship notes) that the reader will want to know when, how, why, and for whom particular books were originally written. We can get something out of them even if we ignore all these questions, but what we get will risk being vague and muddled. But in recent years these assumptions have been challenged by two movements which are in many ways radically opposed, but have become strange bedfellows in opposing the traditional task of biblical study as I have been describing it.

For a long time it has been customary for more conservative writers on the Bible to stress the limitations of any approach that treats biblical books as composite entities, composed of many strands that developed over a long period of time. Even if this is true, it is said the *canonical* Scriptures for Christians are the finished products: 2 Samuel, not 'the Succession Narrative'; Isaiah, not various fragmentary bits of Isaiah 1–39; Genesis, not just one strand in Genesis; the Gospel according to Matthew, not some hypothetical source underlying Matthew. When God inspired the Church to recognise the books of the Old and New Testaments as the exclusive Scriptures for the Christian community, he meant us to read the books in their finished form. Some 'fundamentalist' Christians, it is true, have spent a lot of time actually attacking (with much sophistication) the idea that biblical books are composite. But most more conservative Christians (Protestant or Catholic) are willing to entertain the idea that a long history of editing and re-editing lies behind the books we now have: they just do not think it matters. Whatever the historical process behind the Bible may have been, it is its end product that enshrines divine revelation. And it is therefore the end product that should be the basis for interpretation. Hypothetical earlier 'sources' are of quite secondary interest.

In the last few years this way of thinking has received an enormous boost from a most unexpected quarter;

secular literary criticism. Traditionally, literary critics have not been much interested in the Bible, except in the language of the Authorised Version. Building on a traditional element within the church itself, they have seen the Bible as religiously important but not high in purely literary merit, and most have agreed with C.S. Lewis:

> There is a certain sense in which 'the Bible as literature' does not exist. It is a collection of books so widely different in period, kind, language, and aesthetic value, that no common criticism can be practised on them. In uniting these heterogeneous texts the Church was not guided by literary principles, and the literary critic might regard their inclusion between the same boards as a theological and historical accident irrelevant to his own branch of study.[11]

> Unless the religious claims of the Bible are again acknowledged, its literary claims will, I think, be given only 'mouth honour' and that decreasingly . . . In most parts of the Bible everything is implicitly or explicitly introduced with 'Thus saith the Lord'. It is . . . not merely a sacred book but a book so remorselessly and continuously sacred that it does not invite, it excludes or repels, the merely aesthetic approach. You can read it as literature only by a *tour de force*. You are cutting the wood against the grain, using the tool for a purpose it was not intended to serve.[12]

In the last twenty years or so, however, literary critics have become very interested in the Bible. Outstanding examples are Frank Kermode, *The Genesis of Secrecy* (Cambridge, Mass. 1979), on the Gospel according to St Mark; Robert Alter, *The Art of Biblical Narrative*

(London 1981) and *The Art of Biblical Poetry* (New York 1985); *The Literary Guide to the Bible* (Cambridge, Mass. 1987) edited by these two scholars jointly; Gabriel Josipovici, *The Book of God* (New Haven and London 1988); Harold Bloom, *The Book of J*, (New York 1990); and Northrop Frye, *The Great Code: the Bible and Literature* (London, Melbourne, and Henley 1981). The *Literary Guide* draws on a considerable range of secular literary critics and biblical scholars receptive to 'the Bible as Literature'.

It happens that this renewed interest in the literary merit of the Bible arrived after a time in which the world of literature had been rather hostile (for its own reasons) to the fragmentation of literary works. Its watchword had been 'Read what is set before you.' Speculations on the psychology of the author, the time and place of writing, or even the author's intentions, had tended to be outlawed; and a kind of formalism won the day, in which the work in itself, rather than anything outside it, is the proper object for interpretation. So when secular critics approach the Bible, many of them do so with a prior commitment to the view that the text exactly as it stands is what criticism should interpret. Northrop Frye, for example, in *The Great Code*, treats the whole Bible (Old and New Testaments) as if it were a single literary work, in which Genesis 1 and Revelation 22 are the natural beginning and end. Within this work we can detect connections and patterns between the individual books without any regard to merely 'historical' questions about the component parts. The Bible, just as it is (which tends also to mean: in the Authorised Version) is the central literary document of Western culture. What bits of it may have meant to wandering tribesmen or early church leaders is neither here nor there. Similarly in the *Literary Guide to* the Bible most contributors ask about the literary effect of this or that book on a modern reader, rather than placing it in an historical context.

The result has been a style of secular biblical criticism which reads very much like ultra-conservative Christian or Jewish scholarship. Conservative Christians have not been slow to see the advantages that can accrue to them from making common cause with the secular literary critics. As well as the traditional complaint that 'historical' scholars (the people we called 'the critics' in chapter 4) are irreverent and sceptical, they can now add that such scholars are out of date, and out of touch with 'real' literary criticism. Thus 'critical' scholarship can very easily be presented as a dinosaur struggling to survive after *real* criticism has moved on to much more interesting and important topics. Many books and articles are now written by biblical scholars presenting themselves as 'literary critics', whose real underlying motivation is the conservative one of dodging questions about sources, developments, and inconsistencies within the Bible.

Interestingly, however, there are some signs that secular criticism of the Bible is now coming of age, and in the process becoming willing to admit the old 'critical' questions back into its purview. Gabriel Josipovici's *The Book of God*, though it deals with the whole Bible, is a good way removed from Northrop Frye's work in that it allows questions about dates and authorship. Still more strikingly, for Harold Bloom's *The Book of J* the possibility of separating out the 'J' strand of the Pentateuch is crucial. J is the oldest of the four strands from which the Pentateuch was composed. He argues that the various editors of Genesis were impelled by an 'orthodox' desire to tone down the religiously cool and even impish presentation of God by J, but for us it is vital to penetrate beneath their work and read the 'original' J on its own terms. This is just what biblical scholars have believed for a hundred years, though few have done it with Bloom's quirky humour and literary flair (and occasional wild inaccuracies!)

But it would be just as foolish to say, 'Look, secular critics are now in favour of biblical criticism' as it has been of conservatives to claim them for their camp. Readers of the Bible must make up their own minds which questions it is sensible to ask, and be mature enough to evaluate comments – whether from 'biblical critics' or from 'literary critics' – on their own merits. We should not crave the prestige of being able to line up with some influential person, but should read the text for ourselves. If this book succeeds in persuading its readers to try the Bible for themselves, instead of waiting to be told what to believe about it, I shall have achieved my aim. My intention has been to whet readers' appetites for the text, not to legislate about what they are allowed to find there.

Notes

1 Northrop Frye, *The Great Code: The Bible and Literature* (London, Melbourne, and Henley 1981), pp. xviii–xix.

2 James Barr, *The Scope and Authority of the Bible* (Explorations in Theology 7, London, SCM Press 1980), p. 7.

3 Quotations are from J.B. Pritchard (ed.), *Ancient Near Eastern Texts relating to the Old Testament* (2nd edition, Princeton 1955), p.422.

4 Werner Keller, *The Bible as History. Archaeology Confirms the Book of Books* (London 1956; revised with a postscript by J. Rehork, 1980).

5 Dorothy L. Sayers, 'A Vote of Thanks to Cyrus', in her *Unpopular Opinions* (London 1946), pp. 23–8. The quotations are from pp. 23 & 24.

6 Philip Berryman, *Liberation Theology* (London 1987), pp. 49–50. A mild English version of liberation theology can be found in David Sheppard, *Bias to the Poor* (London 1983).

7 John W. de Gruchy, *The Church Struggle in South Africa* (Grand Rapids and London 1979), pp. 30–1. I am grateful to my colleague Tonia Cope for bringing this book to my attention.

8 Harold Bloom, *The Book of J* (New York 1990), p. 32.

9 Mary Hayter, *The New Eve in Christ: The Use and Abuse of the Bible in the Debate About Women in the Church* (London 1987), p. 18.

10 *Reader's Digest Bible Illustrated*, ed. B.M. Metzger (London, no date); *The One Year Bible* (Tyndale House Publishers, Wheaton, Illinois, 1985); *The Bible in One Year* (International Bible Society, 1988), based on the NIV.

11 C.S. Lewis, 'The Literary Impact of the Authorized Version', in *They Asked for a Paper* (London 1962), pp. 26–50. The quotation is from p. 27.

12 ibid., pp. 48–9.

Appendix 1
The Hebrew Bible

The Law

1 Genesis
2 Exodus
3 Leviticus
4 Numbers
5 Deuteronomy

The Prophets

    The Former Prophets
6 Joshua
7 Judges
8 Samuel
9 Kings

    The Latter Prophets
10 Isaiah
11 Jeremiah
12 Ezekiel
13 The Twelve: Hosea
                 Joel
                 Amos
                 Obadiah
                 Jonah
                 Micah
                 Nahum
                 Habakkuk
                 Zephaniah
                 Haggai
                 Zechariah
                 Malachi

The Writings
14 Psalms
15 Job
16 Proverbs

The Megilloth (scrolls)
17 Ruth
18 Song of Songs
19 Ecclesiastes
20 Lamentations
21 Esther

22 Daniel
23 Ezra-Nehemiah
24 Chronicles

Appendix 2
The Catholic Bible

(Italicized titles are those that appear in the Apocrypha in Protestant Bibles)

The Historical Books

Genesis
Exodus
Leviticus
Numbers
Deuteronomy
Joshua
Judges
1 Samuel
2 Samuel
1 Kings
2 Kings
1 Chronicles
2 Chronicles
Ezra
Nehemiah
Esther *with additions*
Judith
Tobit
1 Maccabees
2 Maccabees

The Poetical Books

Psalms
Proverbs
Ecclesiastes

Song of Songs
Job
Wisdom of Solomon
Ecclesiasticus

The Prophetic Books

Hosea
Amos
Micah
Joel
Obadiah
Jonah
Nahum
Habakkuk
Zephaniah
Haggai
Zechariah
Malachi
Isaiah
Jeremiah
Lamentations
Baruch
The Letter of Jeremiah (= Baruch 6)
Ezekiel
The Story of Susannah (= Daniel 13)
Daniel *with additions: Prayer of Azariah & Song of the*
    Three Holy Children
Bel and the Dragon (= Daniel 14)

Appendix 3

Reading the New Testament in Chronological Order

1 & 2 Thessalonians
1 & 2 Corinthians
Galatians
Romans
Philippians
Colossians
Philemon
Hebrews
Mark
Matthew
James
Revelation
1 Peter
Luke & Acts
Ephesians
1 & 2 Timothy
Titus
John
1, 2, & 3 John
2 Peter
Jude

Reading the Old Testament in Chronological Order

Pre-10th century

Judges 5
2 Samuel 1:17-27
2 Samuel 23:1-7
Deuteronomy 33
Habakkuk 3

10th century

Gen 2-3, 12-50
Exodus 1-24, 32-3
Num 11-14, 21-24

9th century

2 Sam 5-20
1 Kings 1-2
Psalms 8, 29, 46-48, 96-100, 104
Proverbs 22:17-24:22

8th century

Amos
Hosea
Micah 1-3
Isaiah 1-10, 28-31
1 Kings 17-22
2 Kings 1-7

7th century

Deuteronomy 12-26
2 Kings 22-3
Jeremiah 1-23
Habakkuk 1-2

6th century

2 Kings 24-5
Lamentations
Ezekiel 1-18
Psalm 137
Obadiah
Isaiah 40-55

Deuteronomy 32
1 Kings 8
Ezra 5-6
Isaiah 56-66
Ezekiel 20, 36-7
Haggai
Zechariah 1-8
Deuteronomy 1-4, 28-30

5th century

Job
Genesis 1
Exodus 31, 36-9
Leviticus 18-23
Proverbs 1-9

4th-3rd centuries

1 Chronicles 15-17, 22-3, 28-9
Ecclesiastes
Nehemiah
Malachi
Jonah
Ruth
Esther

2nd century

Ecclesiasticus
Daniel
Tobit
Judith

1st century

Wisdom of Solomon

Appendix 4
Reading the Old Testament by Genre

Narratives

Genesis
Exodus 1-24
Numbers 21-24
Judges 13-16
1 & 2 Samuel
1 Kings 1-11, 17-22
2 Kings 1-7
Jeremiah 32-45
Daniel 1-6
Esther
Ruth
Jonah
Tobit

Wisdom

Psalms 1, 37, 49, 73
Proverbs 1-9, 14-17, 30
Ecclesiastes
Ecclesiasticus

Hymnody

Psalms 8, 18, 19, 22-5, 29-30, 33-4, 42-3, 45-8, 51, 62-3, 65-7, 84-6, 89, 91, 95-100, 103-4, 115, 121, 145-50
Judges 5
Habakkuk 3

Deuteronomy 32
1 Samuel 2:1-10
2 Samuel 1:17-27
Isaiah 38:9-20

Prophecy and Apocalyptic

Isaiah
Amos
Micah
Jeremiah 1-31
Zechariah 1-8
Daniel 7-12
Joel